D1488277

Public Goods, Redistribution and Rent Seeking

Public Goods, Redistribution and Rent Seeking

Gordon Tullock

George Mason University, USA

The Locke Institute

Edward Elgar

Cheltenham, UK • Northampton, MA, USA

© Gordon Tullock, 2005

Published by
Edward Elgar Publishing Limited
Glensanda House
Montpellier Parade
Cheltenham
Glos GL50 1UA
UK

Edward Elgar Publishing, Inc.
136 West Street
Suite 202
Northampton
Massachusetts 01060
USA

A catalogue record for this book
is available from the British Library

ISBN 1 84376 637 X (cased)

Printed and bound in Great Britain by MPG Books Ltd, Bodmin, Cornwall

Contents

Preface

I started on this book just as the difficulties with Iraq were beginning to heat up. As a reader will remember, we took quite a while getting ready to move. Thus a sort of war atmosphere was present while I was writing the manuscript. I don't, however, think this had much impact on it. I have a few mentions of the war and of terrorism but they certainly don't dominate the book.

Basically it is a revision and improvement of the public choice literature on why we have a state, and why it would be nice if it worked better. It's easy enough to read so that it could be used for students who have had no introduction to public choice, but I have enough new ideas in it so that it should be of interest to more advanced scholars too.

At the end I propose some fairly radical revisions to the US Constitution intended both to make it fairer by giving citizens of different states equal representation in a revised Senate and making it harder to engage in the kind of rent seeking which tends to make us poorer. The last is rather radical, but I am well known to be radical, albeit in an unusual direction.

1. Some difficulties in the existing theory of externalities

This book carries a title, which may puzzle many readers. Public goods, redistribution, and rent seeking do not seem to be closely enough related to fit together in one book. Further, public goods is a rather misleading name. I normally talk about externalities, rather than public goods. Externalities are the reason that we must have governments and in many cases they lead to discussion of specific government activities, which generate further externalities and hence require further governmental activity. Nevertheless, they are usually not discussed together, nor in general, are redistribution and rent seeking included under the same general heading. I hope to convince the reader that it is logical to talk about them in an integrated way. I shall, however, start with externalities without mentioning that the existence of poor people in the community was listed by Milton Friedman as generating something rather like an externality. That subject will be put off until we reach the redistribution part of the book where its connection with externalities will eventually be made clear. Further, the connection of both with rent seeking will be made clear. I therefore hope that the reader will be a little patient while I go through what he will probably think is a detour before reaching the main themes.

What then is an 'externality'? As the word implies it is something, which occurs as a sort of byproduct of any action. If I mow my lawn, the noise may annoy my neighbor. This is an externality. Similarly if I hire somebody to mow my lawn, this voluntary contract may also noisily annoy my neighbor. This is also an externality. These are private externalities, but it is possible for government to do things, which annoy people who live outside its jurisdiction. War is an obvious case, but there are

1

many much more minor things which governments can do which annoy outsiders. I must deal with even more primitive and fundamental causes of government. We must for this purpose go back to the origin of government, and that was so long ago that we don't really know much about it. Our near relatives, the chimpanzees, live in bands with only the thinnest signs of a government. There are dominance orders in most chimpanzee bands but these do not function as government, merely ensuring that dominant members have special privileges (De Waal 1989, 1992).[1] They frequently have tribal territories about which they fight.[2]

When we turn to the pre-humans we know almost nothing about them except that they lived in bands and had centers to which they returned from time to time. They seem to have accumulated workable stones brought from short distances in those centers, which is how we know. It seems likely that they also had dominant members.

Very primitive tribes also give us clues as to the early history of our species. They usually have certain members whom scholars call 'Chiefs' or 'Matriarchs' and who can obtain special privileges from the others as well as settling disputes among them. It seems likely that people who have special talents in the use of force get general control of these tribes. With development, these tribes might grow in size and even establish permanent locations. Many primitive tribes, however, have a geographical area, which they dominate, but they move around a lot. Some engage in slash and burn agriculture. With the improvement of technology it seems likely that the tribes would get bigger and that the central control, individual or group, would begin to use its power to tax the remaining members and try to keep out other tribes. Thus taxing, policing to prevent competition at the local level, and military force to prevent competition from other tribes, were probably very early elements of these communities.

The oldest cities of which we have knowledge – Katal Huyuk and Jericho are both fortified, albeit rather primitively. It is only with the development of agriculture that permanent settlement became possible. Presumably they originally developed as simple farming villages but cities like Jericho and Katal Huyuk are also very old. There is no doubt that they engaged in considerable trade – Katal Huyuk dealt in obsidian, a very valuable material in the Stone Age. From the remains it would appear that they had a strong religion, but in neither case do we have direct evidence of a central government. Granted the necessity of mobilizing labor to build the heavy walls of Jericho and the peculiar design of Katal Huyuk which seems to be based on defensive considerations, it is fairly certain that they had a central government. We do not know whether it was a simple chief or some kind of consulting group. It seems likely however that they had a chief who was normally a simple extreme example of the dominance found in primitive tribes.

When we move along to literate societies, which started in Mesopotamia, we find that they are based on irrigation agriculture. This requires centralized control and the ability to mobilize large numbers of workers (Wittfogel 1957). In these city-states there were elaborate religious structures that appear also to be centers of government. It is clear from the structures that the government was able to mobilize for its own use a fairly large part of the total wealth of the community. In part this would be a necessity to keep up the irrigation system and in part a necessity to keep out foreign robbers. The earliest evidence that we have about the actual government of these entities are two epic poems about an early king named Gilgamesh. We only have bits and pieces and further what we have is a translation into a later language. The original text is gone. The hero is a king but there is at least some indication of a consultative body of some sort.

When we go to later in the same area, we have much better data and the kings are absolute. It seems likely that the central government such as it was had a monopoly of force (which, we now tend to think, is a distinguishing characteristic of government) and used it for its own benefit. Looking at it from the standpoint of the common citizens, however, the necessity of keeping the irrigation canals functioning meant that the need to mobilize large numbers of workers was obvious. Further, in the early days, there were other such cities in the vicinity. It seems likely that defense against them would have appeared to be necessary to the average citizen. The pomp and ceremony of the religion and the monarch's court probably gave workers at least some entertainment. Modern dictators normally have numerous expensive ceremonies and apparently think that from the standpoint of the dictator they have cost–benefit pay-offs.

With the exception only of irrigation canals, which were apparently not necessary in Jericho and Katal Huyuk, the origin of government in other areas was probably similar. Apparently, somebody with special talents in the organization of violence decided to tax his neighbors (subjects) in order to support him and his mechanism of violence. It seems likely that originally this was to the benefit of the citizens who were protected against theft and invasion. Mancur Olson with his usual ability for the winning phrase referred to the 'stationary bandit' (1982), rather than the 'roving bandit'. The chief or king had strong motives to increase the productivity of his area because much of the product would end up in his hands. This was only true if he intended to stay there while a migratory bandit would simply grab and leave.

That this was the origin of the state seems likely although it was so long ago that we cannot be sure. In the late nineteenth century, anthropologists visiting Africa found a number of things, which they called 'empires'. They were usually quite small; a couple of thousand square miles at most and rather recently created. Their history was much what we have deduced above. Once control over a given tribal area was established, the prevention of competition could be a high priority. Partly this competition would be purely local, individuals stealing their neighbors' property which otherwise could be taxed by the king. Thus the creation of some kind of police force would seem likely. Note that this would benefit most individual citizens as well as a king. We could regard this as the elimination of an externality for the citizens, but that was probably not the main motive from the government standpoint.

Prevention of competition from other tribes would also be a high priority for the ruler. Thus he would develop an army to keep out others and probably to increase his own tax ability by aggression. The defensive part of this use of the army would be a benefit to the citizens and he might have permitted them to loot areas that he conquered so they gained there too. Note that both of these primitive aspects of government to at least some extent benefited the citizens if they could be said to have reduced external costs. It seems unlikely however that that was the motive of, in Mancur Olson's phrase, the 'stationary bandit'.

If he were going to engage in wars of aggression against his neighbors, roads would be useful. The oldest known roads are the ridgeways of England and we have no history to tell us their origin although their utility is obvious. The first major road system was built by the Assyrians, those mighty and aggressive warriors. They built the first large road system to permit their army to get around.[3] When the Assyrians were destroyed, the Persians maintained and expanded their road system. No doubt citizens as well as armies used the roads, but that was a byproduct from the standpoint of the government concerned. An externality was eliminated but that was not the motive of the government. The citizens may have regarded the need to build roads as obvious.

Above the front door of many American post offices is a quotation from Herodotus describing the imperial Persian postal system. It does not seem likely that this very well organized postal service was the first, but it does seem likely that the postal service was originally developed for the purpose of maintaining control of the empire in the hands of its ruler.

Thus, some basic functions of government were developed, not to eliminate externalities but to make government more secure and wealthy. Other people could use the roads and possibly the postal couriers would carry private correspondence as well, but it was not an effort to benefit the citizens but to benefit the government.

The Persians of course were not the last. Those mighty warriors, the Romans, build roads all over their extensive empire. I have walked across a bridge built in the reign of Tiberius. By his time, the roads were not needed for conquest but they were needed to keep the empire together. Chin Shih Huang Ti unified China by military conquest, but he also provided a major road network. The conquering Incas built excellent roads in most unfavorable terrain.

The military significance of roads has continued. Hitler built the autobahn for military purposes and in the 1950s, the US interstate highway system was originally rationalized by President Eisenhower as part of the defense establishment. Of course roads have many other purposes than moving armies and the post office is used more by private citizens than by the government. In fact it appears to be in process of being eliminated by competition from private companies. Nevertheless, the highways' origin was not elimination of externalities but improving the power of the government.

Above, I said that economists normally justify government activity by the elimination, or at least control, of externalities. There is no doubt that much government activity is inspired by that motive. There is also no doubt that much government activity long ago when it first started was not intended to reduce externalities but strengthen the powers of the 'stationary' bandit. We gained from it because he did in fact reduce externalities, including those externalities of an invasion and in present-day times it seems likely that such externalities motivate most government action. That was not true however long, long ago when government started.

There is another possible reason for government that benefits the average citizens in many states but inflicts externalities on citizens of other states. The United States has a Department of Defense, which ironically has never fought a defensive war. We Americans gained a great deal from the continuous minor wars of aggression waged against the Indians and from the major war of aggression against Mexico. Sometimes the wars of aggression were unsuccessful. The war of 1812 did not succeed in conquering Canada. President James Madison, although brilliant in designing constitutions, was an ineffective war president and the military machine had been so weakened by President Thomas Jefferson that it was unable to carry out its initial objectives. In any event we have gained from numerous successful wars, and if we claim that they reduced externalities we are stretching the word a good deal.[4]

Let us now turn to the externalities, which are used by most economists to justify government. If I engage in activity which injures or benefits someone else without his agreement, that is an externality, albeit the person who feels the externality may be happy about it if it is positive. Let me take an example. Suppose at three in the morning I go out on the balcony of my apartment and begin to practice the trumpet. Since my apartment is in a large building and there are a number of other large apartment buildings within 100 yards, there would probably be considerable objection. Indeed the building police (a private police company) would probably appear and make me stop. I have clearly created a negative externality for my fellow dwellers in the apartment complex and the policeman, collectively hired by all of the tenants, is abating that externality. Note that the building being a condominium, and the police being provided by a private company, does not change this matter much. If for some reason the private policeman could not get me to stop, the police provided by the city of Arlington would no doubt take a turn. Indeed I might end up being tried by the regular court.

But suppose I get pleasure out of practicing the trumpet. Is preventing me from doing so an externality generated by the other tenants and injuring me? I am sure most of my readers will think this is a silly question, but why? Comparative numbers is not the explanation. A loud and rowdy party disturbing only one person at three in the morning would also call for police intervention. The apparent explanation here is simply that by the customs of our society, loud noises at three in the morning are a nuisance and to be abated. Ownership of an apartment carries with it a legal right to the absence of annoying noises at three o'clock in the morning. Other societies have other rules. One of the intriguing features of London is the extremely late hours that parties continue. Starting a party at midnight is not totally out of the question.

These are different customs and there is no particular rationale for any of them. The one that is contrary to custom is thought to be a generator of externality while the same amount of noise under other circumstances is not (Coase 1960). There is no way of deciding whether it is an externality except the prevailing customs or the legal situation.

In Basle on one night of the year almost the entire populace goes out and walks in the streets beating on drums. Clearly this is as likely to disturb people's sleep, as is my trumpet. But under the local rules, it is perfectly legal, indeed approved, so that someone who did not do this, particularly if they had small children, would get a certain amount of social disapproval.

I have a number of libertarian friends. They object to the use of force and violence or the threat implied by a policeman and look for voluntary ways to dealing with such problems. Suppose that instead of hiring a policeman my neighbors had got together and paid me to stop. I imagine the per capita payment needed would not be much more than the cost of maintaining the police, and might well be substantially less. Further note that no one is injured. I gain because I prefer the fee and my neighbors gain because the cost is, probably, less than hiring a policeman. Nevertheless I am sure most of my readers will think that this is a silly proposal.

Why? The answer is fairly simple and is called 'free riding' by professional economists (Olson 1965). If my neighbors formed a coalition to pay me not to play the trumpet, any individual could get the same benefit if he did not join the coalition and hence did not put in any money. This would reduce the total payment only trivially and presumably leave enough money from the others to stop my playing the trumpet. This is obvious but we would all assume that it would be impossible to actually form the coalition because many of my neighbors would choose to free ride on the gifts of the others. This would increase the payments needed by those who were making contributions and hence magnify the motive for abstaining. Further, if my moral principles were weak, I might play the trumpet solely in order to procure payments designed to make me stop.

This is not the only case of this kind. Indeed the prospect of this kind of free riding is normally used to explain the need of government compulsion. Things like the payment to not play the trumpet at three in the morning are rather misleadingly called 'public goods'. I did not invent this usage and would prefer some other phrase, but this is what you will find in most economics books.

Let me go through a few other cases. When I moved into my house in Tucson, Arizona, I discovered that eta ants (sometimes called parasol ants) had a nest in my backyard. These ants, probably the most developed of the ant family, take small pieces of leaves off trees and other plants, carry them to their nests (hence the name parasol ants) and chew them up and raise mushrooms on them. These mushrooms are the sole food of these ants. Since they can strip almost any plant, including trees, of their leaves, they are a decided nuisance. In addition they are very hard to kill off. If poison is put on the ground near the entrance of their nests, they stay inside eating the mushrooms and they create an alternative entrance.

At the time I moved in, it was a small nest and had not damaged the plants of my neighbors, but this was obviously merely a matter of time. Was this is externality? I am not an environmentalist, but I am interested in social insects. I might have kept them to study. Would this be an externality? And if my neighbors had complained vigorously and audibly, would their complaints be an externality? Suppose my neighbors were environmentalists and objected to changing the balance of nature. If I wanted to eliminate the ants in order to protect my own garden, these neighbors presumably would object. To make it more complicated there are environmentalists who are protective of plants not animals. They might think that killing these ants was environmentally required. What is the externality?

I had other difficulties with social insects. It turned out that another native species, termites, were living under the concrete slab on which my house stood and beginning to eat the wooden parts of the house. Ignoring environmental concerns, I called an exterminator who proceeded to take care of the problem by poisoning them. He reported, however, that he could not find the nests and thought it might be under the other part of the concrete slab upon which my house was built. There were two houses sharing a common wall and on the same slab. My neighbors were reluctant to do anything about the termites. Was it then an externality? And if so was I inflicting it on them, or they inflicting it on me? Fortunately for me, the exterminator company had a very persuasive salesman who succeeded in selling them an extermination job.

The development, which had been built into a condominium by a real estate company, was on the side of the hill with a very pretty view across the city of Tucson to the mountains beyond. There were some trees already in existence and the real estate company planted more. With time they got bigger and began interfering with the view of some of the houses. I was fortunate in that they in essence improved my view because they were not directly between my house and the city. It happened that the real estate company had realized this might happen and put in our charter a provision that trees, which interfered with the view, could be cut down. This provision, of course, could be changed by the 'government' of the condominium. It turned out some people wanted some trees cut down and others were firmly in favor of preserving them. In this case the squabble was carried on within the elected government and at annual meetings. Was the externality the trees, the view, or the disturbances in governmental meetings that the problem raised?

Tucson, being on the edge of the tropics, there were certain noxious insects about. Several times I exterminated small colonies of black widow spiders. Returning to the environmentalists, some of them might have objected to my reducing the variety of species in the area by killing termites and eta ants. I don't think that environmentalists ever object to killing black widow spiders in inhabited areas, particularly where there are children. Nevertheless it is quite possible that, even there, I was inflicting externalities on environmentalists who object to the extermination of any species or even radical changes in the 'state of nature'.

There are other more complicated cases. In my front yard I had a night-blooming *Cereus*. For those who have not seen them, this has white flowers five to six inches across which open about 7:00 in the evening and close at dawn. The individual bloom lasts only that one night, but the cactus upon which it blooms will produce more such flowers for quite a while during the summer. My neighbors used to admire my flowers and would occasionally take pictures or invite their guests to come and look. This can be called a positive externality since my activity in leaving the cactus in place benefited my neighbors. Unfortunately, this particular flowering cactus is fertilized by bats. I remember my surprise at looking into the flower and seeing a bat drinking the nectar. But there are some people who dislike bats, especially when they are rabid. My cactus attracted bats. Was it then generating a negative externality that more than counterbalanced the positive externality produced by its appearance? It could be producing positive externalities for some people and negative for others.

Of course we could subsidize people who produce beautiful gardens for the benefit of their neighbors and passersby. Some neighborhoods have little contests with a prize for the most attractive yard. The particular condominium that I lived in Tucson did not have such prizes, but they did have rather strict rules on what you could have in your front yard. It had to be native desert plants and you could not raise grass. The back yard, which was generally invisible because of a wall, was free for anything you wished to raise. Except for the grass, which was banned by the county government in order to conserve water, these rules were strictly local. The idea was to improve the general appearance of the neighborhood and to keep up the resale price of the houses. There were also restrictions on the house design for the same reason. The result was a very generally pleasant appearance and good resale values on houses.

I used to live in Blacksburg, Virginia, where the dogwoods

were particularly beautiful in the spring. I used to drive out of my way in order to pass by a house with a spectacular display of dogwoods in the spring. The owner of the house was generating a positive externality, or perhaps a negative externality, on their neighbors who had to put up with considerable excess traffic.

Returning to Tucson and the rules of my condominium, in a part these rules involved the color of the house and all houses were made of the same type of brick. One new arrival purchased an empty lot and began building a house using a different color brick. The condominium association warned him about this, eventually sued him and collected $7000. Was he generating an externality or was the condominium association generating an externality by first criticizing seriously and then suing? How about the regulation on the color of my house? Suppose that I would prefer another color. Are they imposing a negative externality on me?

At the time that I was writing this chapter the United States was full of prominently displayed American flags as a result of the terrorist attacks on the World Trade Center. A Mrs. Parrot erected a ten-foot flagpole in her front yard, landscaped its base and raised an American flag. She was a citizen of a condominium, which had a rule against flagpoles in the yard although not those attached to the house. Rather to my astonishment, and that of most other people, I suspect, the condominium association began legal proceedings against her. Her immediate neighbors did not object to the flag and in the current patriotic mood it seems unlikely that anybody much really objected. Nevertheless the condominium association governors objected and sued.[5]

I suspect that most of my readers, have, in each case, made their decision as to whether these are externalities fairly easily. A little experimentation, however, has shown that different people make different decisions. Further, when people engage in careful thought about one of these problems, they tend to change their mind and then after further thought change back, etc. Since these problems are not very important, it is not worthwhile spending a lot of time worrying about them.

Nevertheless the fact that people do reach different decisions and change their minds indicates there is no straightforward rule for controlling them.

In general, these problems either are dealt with informally by discussion, sometimes very acerbic discussion, or referred to some governmental agents. Sometimes, they will be referred to an arbitrator who is usually simply some prominent person in the area. It is not true however that this always resolves the problem. The parties may be dissatisfied and perhaps regard the decision by the government or an arbitrator as inflicting negative externality upon them.

Government is not a final solution, because governments sometimes inflict externalities. These may be inflicted on a minority within the government's area or outside. The reader may think that the word 'externality' should not be used if it is a government agency and the victim is a member of the community. This is simply a question of word usage. Bombing of cities in a foreign country would be clearly an externality, but it is not custom to deal with war in these terms. Thus our imposing a no-flight rule on about two-thirds of Iraq may be objected to or approved of without considering whether it was or was not an externality. I suppose that the bombing of the World Trade Center was strictly speaking, an externality imposed by one lunatic religious group. I do not think however that that is the way the problem is looked at by most people and from now on I will follow common usage in this case.

Let me look at simple examples of governmental units inflicting externalities on people outside that unit. Once again, I turn to the condominium development in which I lived in Tucson. Some years before this condominium was constructed a small development had been built in which a minor road with a couple of offshoots had been constructed connecting to a major street. The idea was to provide space for house building, and people in fact bought lots and built houses. They had a tiny collective organization for the 25 or so houses.

When the real estate firm, which built the condominium in which I lived, started it, its street system was connected to two major streets. In one case, the less important, the connection was by way of the street built by the previous developer for the small colony of houses built on his lots. As it turned out this entrance was used a good deal with the result that there was fairly heavy traffic through the small development. Since a number of these houses had children who might be run over and all of them objected to the noise and other disturbances caused by this traffic, they decided to cut the use of 'their' road by blocking the end of it. The condominium dwellers objected and took the matter up with the county government. Since they outnumbered the voters living on the short road by twenty to one, the county government sided with them. Clearly the large number of voters in this case chose to inflict an externality on the few.

As a general proposition, in democratic states the majority may, and frequently does, inflict costs on minorities. The high taxes on the wealthy are an obvious example. Is this an externality? If the wealthy live in the same community with the poor, some would probably say that it is not. On the other hand, the Southern Blacks before 1864 lived in the same communities with the whites and some would say that the laws imposing slavery were generating externalities. Once again in this case I shall simply leave the matter aside for a few paragraphs on the grounds that common speech does not use 'externalities' in that way. Since I have in various cases above rather stretched the meaning of 'externality' the reader may object to my not stretching it here. If so, with very little difficulty he or she can use the words as they wish.

There is however a serious difficulty with this definition. It is frequently argued that externalities are a major justification for government. The government can in many cases deal with externalities by imposing a rule. There are two problems here. In the first place a government rule may be the one which imposes externalities, as in the road case above. In many cases the government rule simply provides that one of the two sides who have a disagreement about something, say the termites, must follow a particular rule. Assuming the government is capable of enforcing its decrees, this eliminates the possibility of fighting or quarreling about it, but it does so by inconveniencing one of the parties in order to benefit the other. Obviously, we must on occasion accept this outcome, but it does not really cure the externality. It merely says that one party may inflict the externality on the other. This may be a reasonably satisfactory outcome, but it is an outcome that does not eliminate the problem.

In fact, there may be externalities within the government. Returning once again to the condominium in Tucson, in addition to private gardens, there were some common areas, which were gardened by a contract gardener. One very aggressive member of the little society became convinced that the gardener was doing a bad job. He then began a vigorous one-man campaign to get further work done. He annoyed the president of the society and the members of the various boards by telephone calls and personal visits and circulated manifestoes on the subject. Eventually, the president of the society resigned in order to spare herself from his visits and phone calls. At the time when I left the area, his campaign was still going on and it would be possible to argue that there had been some improvement in the gardening in the common areas.

My impression is that although this was an extreme example, internal disputes within government agencies produce something that is very similar to an externality even if that word is not normally used. Normally, of course, disputes within very small government agencies like our condominiums are settled relatively peacefully. They frequently leave a residue of ill feeling on one side or the other. With larger groups the ill feeling may be extreme and long lasting. For many people the Civil War is not yet over.

In many cases, of course, once a government has made a decision on such a matter, people entering the area later will have to take it into account and this may in fact reduce the externalities. Returning to my condominium development in Tucson, the decision as to the color of the houses means that anyone building a new house who prefers some other color will have to regard the rule as part of his initial contract. It could be argued it is then not an externality because the parties have agreed to it. Most legislation in larger and more important governments has this effect. At the time the law was passed, the mere passage of the law may inconvenience some people while benefiting the others. In normal speech this is not referred to as an externality, but it meets the usual definition. One person's action, pushing for the law, may injure or benefit another person. If a group of people, who are a majority, push a particular law they may inflict considerable costs on the minority. Of course they may also confer benefit on the minority if the minority mistakenly opposed the law through stupidity or misinformation.

Another case in which governments do not cure externalities is when the interests of two groups located in separate governments conflict. The above case of the road is a minor example. World War II is a major example. If there is a supervening power, the matter can be dealt with by it, but with the same problems of majority and minority or powerful and weak that we met in the previous case of local governments. Further the externality may be purely governmental. Although we in the US have tried to prevent states from fighting each other, in at least one important case in 1860–65 we failed, with the result of one set of states imposing a severe externality on another. In this case, of course, we currently look back on the outcome as desirable although that was not necessarily the unanimous view at the time. International wars are even more conspicuous examples of externalities inflicted by governments.

As can be seen from the previous parts of this chapter, the problem of externality is not an easy one. Most economists regard government as existing to a large extent to cure externalities. It certainly does; but it also creates externalities. These externalities may be inflicted on foreigners, people who are outside the jurisdiction of the government. When the government inflicts harm or confers benefit on its own citizens the word 'externality' is normally not used, but that is merely a convention.

Notes

1. The 1989 book, *Peacemaking Among Primates*, is rather mis-titled in the sense that its high point is a particularly vicious murder.
2. Jane Goodall thought chimpanzees were peaceful until she observed a war of extermination by one band against another.
3. 'The Assyrians came down like a wolf on the fold and their hosts were all gleaming in silver and gold,' from Lord Byron's *The Destruction of Sennacherib*.
4. This will be dealt with in more detail later.
5. See *Washington Times*, 8 December 2002, p. A11.

2. Coase and all that

Economists sometimes say that Coase (1960) solved the problem of externalities. While I do not begrudge him his Nobel prize, I have to point out that what he did was clarify the problem, not finally solve it. In a way he simply demonstrated that Pigou, at the time the standard authority on externalities, had misunderstood the problem.

Pigou said that private property alone would not necessarily lead to an optimal outcome. Government action was frequently necessary. Individual actions may impose costs on other individuals and hence we need a government to deal with it. So far Pigou (1929) is clearly right, although it is not obvious that he went far beyond Adam Smith. In a way what he did was clarify the reasoning in an area where earlier economics had generally understood the problem, but not clearly stated it.

But if the market and private property do not lead to an optimal outcome because of externalities, that does not prove that governments will do better. We look at the early history of governments and notice that they were largely forceful efforts to transfer resources to powerful people. Those mighty warriors and builders, the Assyrians destroyed the bulk of the Israelite state. Only the small Southern fragment centered on Jerusalem escaped them, and that was not because of good government, but because of a fortuitous outbreak of plague, which frightened them away. Later of course, Jerusalem itself was taken by another government, the Babylonians, who took the bulk of the population off to the center of the Tigris and Euphrates valley. This again did not reduce externalities, but more accurately created them.

Turning to modern times, this chapter was begun in the aftermath of the second Iraqi war. The motive for the war involves at least claims that it will reduce externalities inflicted upon the United States by terrorists. Whether it will turn out that this war solves a terrorist problem is currently uncertain, but I doubt it. In any event there is no doubt that we have inflicted significant externalities upon the Iraqi people to say nothing of their government. It may be of course that the positive externalities derived by the elimination of one of the worst governments in the world, which was persecuting the Iraqi people, will turn out the more important than the negative externalities. Only time will tell.

As a bit of light relief, may I point out another minor externality connected with that war. As a result of my rather peculiar education and background I am much interested in foreign policy and in military matters. I had no particular objection to the Iraqi war per se, but I thought we had provided far fewer troops than were desirable. I knew how bad the quality of the Iraqi army was, but it did seem to me that we shouldn't take the risk that perhaps at least a few divisions of it, the Presidential Guard, for example, had improved. I feared that we might be temporarily stalled. Thus, in a way, our campaign inflicted a negative externality on me. I take it every single reader will think that the government was correct in paying no attention. Indeed, of course, the government never even knew that I objected to their policy and, strictly speaking, wasting resources in finding out what an obscure professor of economics thought about the matter would indeed have been a waste. Still, there was an externality in the pure sense, and it was generated by the government.

But then, what do we mean by externality? Each of us is surrounded by a vast variety of things some of which are material but some of which are immaterial like for example, the rules to which we are compelled to pay attention. To take two very minor examples, when I entered my office this morning I noticed that some very pretty purple flowers had come into bloom. I also noticed that a bush on the other side of the entrance walk was showing signs of deterioration. I got pleasure from the beautiful flowers and pain from the deterioration: in both cases the amount was so trivial that I didn't even slow down to look. I know that the university administration has planted these things with the idea of improving the functioning of the university, but the effect must be trivial. Nevertheless a decision to have no flowers would probably be unwise. This is a deliberate effort to generate a positive externality by a government.

To say that governments exist to a large extent to 'internalize externalities' is orthodox, and part of modern elementary training in economics. It is one of the theses of this book that the matter is much more complicated. In some of the cases I have given above, governments created externalities. These are not unique or unusual cases. Governments can create externalities. Indeed they may create an externality in the process of dealing with another externality. As a specialist in public choice I am fully familiar with the arguments here and do not deny that we need government in order to avoid or, at least, reduce externalities, but it does other things.

Externalities are extremely diverse. To reiterate, in some cases they come from the actions of individuals or small groups. In other cases they come from the actions of governments. Further in some cases a government acting to reduce a given externality may create another, possibly more severe. Let us go back to Coase (1960) and Pigou (1929). Pigou had pointed out that a railroad locomotive in the technology of his day produced sparks which might start fires in the wheat fields along the right-of-way. He felt that this required government action to minimize this 'externality'. Coase (1960), who was not a great admirer of Pigou, pointed out that in fact it was government action that caused this particular problem. Under common law, a producer of sparks was liable for any damage they might cause. In order to encourage the construction of railroads, Parliament had changed this rule and put the costs on whoever was injured by a fire caused by sparks emitted by a railroad engine. This did not, of course, eliminate the externality. Whichever way the law allocated the damage there was an externality since the fire would in any event cause damage.

The fire danger could be reduced if the locomotive was

equipped with a spark catcher. It could also be reduced if the farmer left an area along the tracks barren or planted with crops which would not burn. Presumably one or the other was the most economical way of reducing the danger. Coase said out that no matter what the law provided, the solution would be the most economical one. If the farmer was liable for the damage and it was cheaper to put a spark arrester on the loco-motives, the farmer would pay the railroad company to install one. If it were cheaper to simply leave a strip along the railroad line barren or planted in crops that would not burn, that would be done either by the farmer if he bore the liability directly or he would be hired by the railroad company to leave the area unfarmed if they bore the liability.

But even with this very simple example Coase can be accused of oversimplification. If the railroad company must hire the farmer to avoid planting burnable crops along the right-of-way, there will be at least some negotiation costs involved. It should also be pointed out that rent seeking[1] comes in here. Whatever the rule, it is no doubt the outcome of political maneuvering, and resources are put into that also. Thus there is no costless solution when the actions of one person or entity affect another. Since such effects are omnipresent in the real world, a truly perfect solution in the sense of one which has no cost, is unlikely. All we can aim at is low cost not no cost.

There is however another more important difficulty. Suppose that the railroad company proposes to hire the farmers to raise crops that will not burn. It must make a deal with each individ-ual farmer. Any individual farmer who insisted on being paid more than the others would make a profit. It might well be that if the railroad company pays most farmers $10 but if one holds out for $50 the sum total would still be an amount low enough so that the railroad company would be willing to pay. But this assumes that the other farmers do not attempt to get $50 them-selves. If the one farmer holds out for his $50 the bargain may fail because others will copy him. Further we would probably expect that that would be the outcome.

On the other hand suppose that the farmers decide to pay the railroad to install a spark catcher. The same problem occurs here. Even though the benefit to the farmers is great enough so that it would be profitable if they each pay the same amount or if the amount depended on the distance from the railroad, individual farmers could gain by refusing to pay and hoping that the others will provide this spark catcher. The simple Coase solution to the problem assumes that there is no bargaining cost and no holdout problem. That seems unlikely.

Long ago, in the simple governments in Mesopotamia, individual bargaining was common. Farmer Jones for example would like to get some wheat and has more cows than he needs. Farmer Smith on the other hand would like an additional cow and is willing to trade wheat for it. After some bargaining they reached tentative agreement on five bags of wheat for the cow. But there is another person involved, farmer Brown would also like the cow and if Smith had not made the offer Jones would have sold for four bags. Thus we can say that the bargain between Smith and Jones injures Brown. We do not call this an externality. Why not?

The explanation is simple and obviously was discovered many centuries ago. We believe that if each person gets the best bargain he can, the net outcome is efficient. Smith has more need of the cow than Brown and society will be better off if he gets it. The word 'externality' is not used here although clearly there is a third person that was injured by the bargain. I take it all my readers will agree that the cow should go to Smith.

The grammatical rule that we do not say that Smith injured Brown externally is just that, a grammatical rule which points to the fact that the outcome is efficient. That private bargains normally lead to efficiency was discovered long ago. But it only applies when the bargaining situation is proper. In the case of the railroad and the farmers, bargaining might not lead to an efficient solution.

Let us return to Coase (1960) and take one of his more amusing examples. Although it looks as if it was made up for amusement or instruction, it is actually drawn from a real English case. There was a doctor who owned a home and yard next door to a factory, which used noisy machinery. At first the doctor was not particularly inconvenienced by the noise, but eventually he decided to build a consulting room in his backyard and the noise made it impossible for him to properly diagnose patients. He sued requesting that the factory be required to operate more quietly. This would be expensive although probably not impossible, so the factory hired a lawyer and tried to defeat the suit.

The problem is a difficult one. The factory noise caused no great difficulty until the doctor built the consulting room in his backyard. It was the doctor who changed the status quo, not the factory. In essence the doctor was saying that he had an implicit right to silence even though until he built a consulting room it was a matter of no importance to him. We can think that the person who moves is the one who in reality causes the externality. There is a doctrine called 'coming to nuisance' which implies that the person who moved is responsible, and this appears to be a particularly clear case. The court however held otherwise and made the factory responsible. I am happy that I did not have to decide this case because it seems to me very difficult. Perhaps making a loud objectionable noise when there is nobody to listen is in a way a minor abuse of privilege and other people are free to move in and hence be inconvenienced and compel the person who has not changed his behavior to do so.

Note that it is not obvious that these two parties are the only people involved in creating the externalities. It could be argued that the title system was wrong and that every piece of property should be regarded as having a sort of belt just inside its legal boundary in which neighboring property has rights. For example, most cities, and the common law in Great Britain, have rules about large buildings, which cut off the light of neighboring property. In essence the property shrinks, as you get higher up. In the above case of the noisy factory it could be argued that the true externality involved here was on the part of the people who originally drew up the land laws without these protections. In general, but with many specific exceptions, you cannot sue governments, but this may be a defect in our law. Indeed it could be argued that even our basic constitutional order inflicts externalities on people whose real estate titles cannot protect them against other kinds of externality. It is possible to regard a defect in the real estate law of title which permits an externality as being itself an externality created by the people who wrote the law.

But we must draw the line somewhere. In a sense the gentlemen who met in Philadelphia created externalities when they drew up the Constitution in such a way that the legal system that came from it would permit laws which limited protection. On the other hand if protection was unlimited, this could also be argued as creating externalities hundreds of years in the future. Note once again that externalities can be positive as well as negative. I would argue that the Philadelphia convention created external benefits and costs for people who not only were not there, but were not alive and might, 200 years in the future, live in areas that were not subject to the jurisdiction of that convention at the time. It is impossible to take every effect, positive or negative, now or in the future, into account.

If we arrange potential externalities from the most important affecting a given person or piece of land to the most trivial we would obtain a bell-shaped curve. We could for example put positive externalities on the right and negative on the left as in Figure 2.1. Certainly it would be wise to ignore the very minor or distant externalities, which we do, but there is no non-arbitrary way of

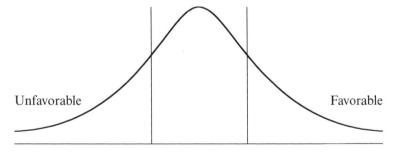

Figure 2.1   Normal distribution of gains and losses

deciding how far out we should go. We can obviously say that Madison's descendants are immune from suits by people who claim the Constitution injured them. Perhaps if impoverished descendants of the Constitution framers argued that we were benefiting from positive externalities from their ancestors' acts we might be sympathetic. Anything we did to help, however, would be an act of sympathy not a legal duty.

Economists in general like diagrams and so I display a normal curve of externality effects on some person or persons from some set of acts. Favorable externalities are on the right and unfavorable on the left. I have drawn two arbitrary vertical lines which are intended to show the point where legal obligation stops and we leave the matter unremedied or unrewarded.

That we must have some such termination in mind when we make decisions in this matter is plain. We live in the world in which we depend very heavily on other people, not only those with whom we have contact but people with whom we have no direct contact.

We can think of the world as composed of physical objects, some of which are people, some inanimate objects. Some of these people or objects have effects on us either direct or indirect. In many cases we regard these as very favorable. In other cases we would rather they were not there and of course the vast majority have no significant effect on us at all. The legal system, if it is to take externalities into account, must classify all of these so that we can prevent or limit negative externalities which fall to the left of one vertical line and get the positive externalities which are on the right of the other. I suppose none of my readers will actually expect that our legal institutions or for that matter, informal controls, will get this perfectly correct.

But why do we turn to the government for dealing with externalities? The explanation is simple. The government is the authorized body for the use of force. They have a police force and an army, which is organized to exert force on people who are reluctant to carry out externality-reducing activities. This is a hangover from the earlier society previously mentioned in this study on the origin of the state and the probability is that it began, in Olson's (1982) phrase as a 'stationary bandit'. It still has these powers and anyone filling out his income tax is apt to feel that it uses them excessively. But we do need in our society both the police and military. In those parts of Washington D.C. where the police cannot exercise complete control there are other organizations providing violence and this is much less satisfactory than the police. Indeed we hope the police will one day suppress these other violence providers. The police and army are supposed to make use of force and threats of force for good ends. We do not expect that from gangs.

But why does the stationary bandit enforce these contracts rather than simply grabbing both the wheat and the cow? The answer is simply that he has a motive to maximize the total wealth of his subject people. He wants them to feel that they can keep things they produce and that efficient work whether in farming or in bargaining will lead to their being better off. Like the modern criminal groups who control a given neighborhood, he has every reason to want his subject and economy to be productive and he remembers the biblical maxim: 'Muzzle not the ox when he treadeth out the corn'.[2] As far as we can tell most kingdoms are internally peaceful and the gains are generally widespread. Much of our present law descends from the Code of Hummurabi. The King and his subjects had strong motives to maintain a peaceful system in which the peasant would be rewarded for his labor and bargains would be kept. The same can be said of our present society.

Notes

1. Rent seeking was first discussed systematically by Tullock (1967). The term 'rent seeking' was first used to describe the activity in question by Krueger (1974). Tullock (1967) described a community of 100 farmers in which access to the main highway is via small trunk roads, each of which serves only four to five farmers. The issue comes up as to whether the entire community of 100 should finance the repair of all of the trunk roads out of a tax on the entire community. Obviously one can envisage a level of repairs and set of taxes on the individual farmers under which such a proposal would be unanimously adopted. But under majority rule it is to the greater advantage of some to propose that only one half of the

roads are repaired out of a tax falling on the entire population. Thus, one can envisage a coalition of 51 of the farmers forming, and proposing that only the roads serving them are repaired out of the community's general tax revenue. Such a proposal would pass under majority rule, and obviously involves a redistribution from the 49 farmers who pay taxes and receive no road repairs, to the 51 farmers whose taxes cover only slightly more than one half of the cost of the road repair.

2. (1 Timothy 5:18), from the King James version of the Bible, New York: Thomas Nelson and Sons.

3. More on why government?

So far we have talked about externalities and a general position that calls for government action with a real or implied threat of force has been presented, but no real reason why the threat of force is necessary. In practice, of course, externalities of a minor sort are frequently dealt with informally without any government activity at all. The termites, which I mentioned earlier, had no government connection, but there are places in the world where legal action to compel people to keep termites under control is the solution selected. Laws against insect pests, which require landowners to keep their land free of some particular species, are not unknown. This is more common with disease carriers than with termites. Nevertheless, this use of government is not rare.

But if sometimes we do use government control, the question is why? It cannot be simply that the government control is used for important matters and informal control for unimportant because some areas where government control is used are not very important. In most American cities if we go to the part where there are individual homes, there will be a building line. This is a rule that all houses must be a certain distance back from the street. Clearly this is not an important matter, although it is obvious that most of the householders will favor it. The use of a single color brick as in my condominium in Tucson is generally favored by the householders, but is a private arrangement not a government one.

In order to explain why we sometimes need government-provided force, let me turn to an incident, which occurred, or more precisely did not occur, in an area of Arlington not far from where I live. The Washington Metro was under construction and a station was proposed for Clarendon. At the time there was a very small cluster of shops there, but basically it was a residential area with a large number of small single family homes. It occurred to some citizens that if these houses were all combined into one large plot it would be possible to build a shopping center with the results that the householders would receive much more than the price they could get by selling the houses one at a time.

The reader has no doubt noticed that shopping centers are normally located rather inconveniently in the outskirts of cities rather than in the center where transportation is easy. The reason is simple. Once land has been broken up into small pieces it is expensive to reassemble them. We have a holdout problem. If the land is put together into one large block the portion under any given house is worth much more than it would be if the land was still disassembled. Thus there are large profits from assembling the land, and this is indeed a specialty of some real estate companies. Normally however, as in the case of Clarendon, if there are many small landholders, assembly is impossible without the use or threat of force. The basic problem is that the persons who hold out for better terms prevent the unanimous agreement necessary for the joint profit.

What happened in Clarendon will, I suppose, surprise no one. A society was set up to collect the titles of all the properties and sell them as a unit. It then occurred to a number of individual householders that they could get more if they held out. This would of course only be true if the rest of the householders stayed in the collective organization. The temptation was too great, and the collective organization broke down. The area is still unconsolidated, although a number of separate big buildings have been built on parts of it.

Not too long ago in connection with reforms that were mainly pushed by the political left, the government was brought into such areas. It was called 'urban redevelopment' and led to very considerable profits to those people whose homes or businesses were in the redeveloped area.

The feeling that government exists to carry out agreed-upon actions is an oversimplification. If there were general agreement no government would be necessary. The reason government exists is that on occasion (frequently) the agreement is incomplete. Temporarily talking about democracies, if most people agree, but some do not, there must be some method of compelling everyone to take the required action, or in some cases, the required inaction. It is somewhat easier in dictatorships, but of course we may not approve of the dictatorial outcome. An organization which is authorized to use force or threat of force is thus necessary, and is the government. This is a less attractive reason for government than the desire to carry out unanimous agreements. The problem is that agreements are seldom unanimous. The normal slogans for democracy call for carrying out the majority will. In my first article in this area I pointed out that simple majority voting is likely to lead to over-investment in government action or facilities. As readers may know, I introduced the view that government should have more than majority support instead, two-thirds or three-quarters (Tullock 1969), but my reason was not simply justification for the use of force, but that this larger majority would lead to more effective government. My argument, which was first offered in a paper read at a Southern Economic Association meeting, was sufficiently radical so that I had great difficulty getting it published. It eventually turned up in Italian, but a moderately revised version was included as an important part of *The Calculus of Consent* (Buchanan and Tullock 1965).

We will return to this matter later, but I do not believe that my argument has been accepted by all the students in the field. Indeed when I read in the area I find very strong feelings that majority is the right way to go. Many people think that this is the definition of democracy, although the same people will normally say you need more than a majority to amend the Constitution and approve of unanimity in the case of American juries.

My recommendation here has not had much practical effect. Perhaps that is changing, however. The proposed constitution for the new unified market in Europe will require 55 percent of the national members to approve any legislation. Further, since some of the members are very small, it is required that the 55 percent contain countries whose population makes up 65 percent of the total population of the community. I doubt that my recommendation had any influence on the draftsmen, but in any event I approve heartily.[1]

But let us leave that matter aside for the time being and turn to more general discussion of government. As far as we can tell democracy has been a very unusual form of government. At the moment about half of the world's population live under governments which can be called democratic, but this is exceptional if we look at the broad history of government. There have been at least three upsurges of democratic government in the general European area. Greece and Rome began as democracies although they were eventually integrated into Imperial Rome, and in the late Middle Ages there were many small cities which were run democratically.

We must deviate here, however, in order to discuss what we mean by democracy. I usually use the term to mean a country in which the functional part of the government is elected by a fairly large group of people. Thus I have no difficulty in referring to Athenian or Roman democracy although in both cases the number of voters was much less than the total population. Slaves, women and Metics could not vote in Athens. Further in order to vote you had to go to the Pynx, which must have been impossible for many citizens. The Romans had a number of civil wars over the franchise. They also did not permit everyone to vote. Further, representative government was unknown and you had to go to the Forum to vote, which would be inconvenient, if you happened to live 100 miles from Rome.

My favorite government, Venice, had a hereditary voting class, which made up about 5 percent of the adult males physically resident in Venice. Since they controlled a sizable empire this was an even smaller minority of it. It is sometimes called an 'oligarchy', although not all of the voters were rich. The European empires, democratic at home, normally did not permit their numerous subject peoples to vote for the home government. The political left in both England and France after

World War II was strongly in favor of dissolving their empires, but they never suggested that the subjects of the larger parts of their empires be permitted to elect members of the House of Commons or the assembly in Paris. Granted the fact that the residents of the home countries were much better off than the citizens of the colonies, the reason is obvious. If India had 80 percent of the members in the House of Commons, which its population would deserve, they would certainly have used it to heavily tax the members of the Labour Party who happened to live in England in order to transfer the funds to the very much poorer inhabitants of India. The Labour Party wanted independence for India, not majority rule for the whole empire.

So far as I know there were no places where every adult citizen could vote before the twentieth century. Washington and Lincoln operated in a government in which only a minority of adults could vote. Until Imperial Germany extended the suffrage to women in 1911 voting was an all-male activity almost everywhere. Indeed it is notable that women did better in monarchies than in democracies. Queens were not unknown, but female Presidents were.[2]

It is notable that the United States did not permit women to vote before 1914 and by 1914 the blacks in the South were effectively prevented from voting. Thus it was only in the 1960s that the United States began permitting all adults to vote.

Thus my definition of democracy as a government elected by a substantial number of people is the only definition of which permits us to talk about a significant history of democratic government. Since most people refer to Greek and Roman democracy and the democratic city-states of the Middle Ages, they must have been using my definition rather than government selected by vote of all adults. The last is a new experiment now only a little less than 100 years old.

Using my more general definition of democracy, the fact is that it has not in general lasted a long time. In 400 BCE the Mediterranean was surrounded by a set of city-states, which were by my definition, democracies. This included not only parts of Greece and Rome but also Carthage. They all disappeared. A number of them disappeared because of Roman conquest. Rome itself fell from internal reasons and many of the other city-states appear also to have fallen from internal problems.

The democratically run city-states of the late Middle Ages seem to mainly have failed to defend themselves against neighboring despotisms. Switzerland and a number of other city-states, survived but they were a minority. We tend to think of our present democracy as a permanent condition and for all I know it is. But historic precedents are not very encouraging.

To repeat, if we regard democracy as government by a clear majority of all the adults living in it and who bother to vote, then it is purely a twentieth-century phenomenon. Restricted franchise with, in particular, only men permitted to vote and frequently only some of them, is a characteristic of the pre-twentieth-century democracies. If the reader does not like calling something like Venice a democracy, I trust that he will permit me to use the language slightly differently. There does not seem to be any other term for this broad category of governments. Since they are in any event, very heavily outnumbered by monarchies of one sort or another, it seems unwise to restrict the term to only some of that group and in particular to eliminate all historic experience by restricting it to full franchise democracies. If we do not, we not only have to eliminate Greece, Rome and the medieval city-states, but we have to eliminate the writers of our Constitution and indeed the whole history of the United States up to the 1960s and the UK before 1928 when the last small category of women were enfranchised.

Intermediate definitions of course are possible. In conversation an enthusiastic but conservative advocate of democracy suggested 45 percent of adults. This would not have fitted the United States before women were permitted to vote because the blacks made up more than 10 percent of the adults, but some such formula as 'quite a lot' may do. But we should not quarrel over definitions. Most modern democracies simply let almost all adults vote. Some like Australia, make voting compulsory. Thus the definition problem concerned history and not the presentday world.

The alternative is some kind of despotism. This has been a common form of government over the ages and even today represents about half of the existing governments. If the despot is wise he would probably seek advice from other members of the group which he controlled. Machiavelli said that a prince should always solicit advice, but should strictly reject unsolicited advice. No doubt for a man who wishes to retain power this was good advice. It seems likely that when 'princes' began to find it necessary to accept counsel from people they had not selected, despotism began to be replaced by more widely based governments. Nevertheless historically, restricted franchise democracy was relatively unusual and as I have said, Athens and Rome are examples of a rare phenomenon not something found on every street. Since both of them failed, it is not obvious that this early development of democracy was an improvement. On the other hand, it should be pointed out that many monarchies also failed, not in the sense that they were replaced by democracies but in the sense that one monarch was replaced by another. The beginning of major democracy then is only about 200 years old in the presentday world.[3] Newspapers were about the same age and may be important for democracy. Whether it will last longer than it did in Rome is of course an open question. Flourishing democracies have been replaced in the past and our democracy may suffer the same fate.

If we turn to the other half of the world, the undemocratic half, they are mostly governed by some type of despotism. There are many different types of despotism ranging from government of ancient Imperial China with the bulk of the officials carefully selected by examination, to feudalism in which the officials inherited their jobs and were expected to make up the royal army. I do not intend to go carefully through this vast universe of different governments since this book is about democracies.

It is, however, I think worthwhile to at least look a little bit into the justifications that were used by conscious monarchists, particularly in France. They pointed out that the King, if he were absolute, had no conflict of interest with his country. He was in somewhat the same situation as a young man who inherited a large corporation in capitalism. He would be motivated to maximize the value of that corporation or kingdom, but in both cases he might spend too much money on himself. Further the accidents of genetic inheritance would probably mean that the inheritor either of the kingdom or the company would tend to be less intelligent than the founder. Thus the kingdom might gradually run down or even face an immediate catastrophe. Historically kingdoms have rarely been replaced by another form of government, but dynasties have been quite regularly replaced. The king must worry about his second cousin, not street rioting, or intellectuals favoring democracy. The Wars of the Roses in England are examples of what the king must worry about in monarchies. And of course dynastic struggles involve a breakdown of the monopoly of force, which is vital for governments. This is true no matter how that particular monopoly is controlled. Normally when we think of rent seeking we consider democratic special-interest groups, the money used for political influence, etc. A little thought however, will lead the reader to realize that the same thing happens in the courts of despots. Any reading of the very extensive literature reporting on the French courts will convince the reader that our rent seeking industry is not unique. Despotisms have them too.

But there is no reason to continue to urge the fact that monarchies are not only common historically, but frequently give pretty good governments. I find that most people considering different types of government simply assume that democracy is right while at the same time feeling that certain countries under royal governments did quite well. Gibbon,[4] for example, thought that the happiest period of the human race was during the four successive adopted Emperors of Rome. In my opinion, we should have better reasons for choosing among possible governments than we do have, but this is not particularly relevant to this study. All we have learned so far here is that the reduction of externalities requires some organization which is capable of using force if it cannot negotiate a mutual agreement.

This is one important reason for the desirability of govern-ments. The construction of public works which are sometimes misnamed 'public goods' and the use of its military and police forces to defend against such forces of other sovereigns or aggress against other sovereigns, despotic or democratic, are among its major activities. Some of these we will no doubt approve of and some we shall disapprove, but for the purpose of this particular chapter they are largely irrelevant. Governments do these things and some citizens gain and others lose.

The question of why we turn to the government for dealing with externalities is seldom asked. It would always be possible to simply pay people to stop doing whatever it is that annoys you or to start doing something you expect to please you. The point here is that the payment itself would be an externality. It may be, however, that the government instead of simply carry-ing out its 'duty' of reducing externalities will instead impose one. Let us return to my trumpet playing. Preventing me from playing the trumpet at three in the morning inconveniences me and hence can be called an externality. Most of us would agree that the net effect would be reduction of externalities even if a cost is imposed on me. We apparently have some idea of what 'normality' is and regard establishing that normality as a desir-able act rather than creating externalities. In a way we do not have a right to deviate from 'normality'. But this is not to solve the problem, it merely puts it in different words.

Readers of history will recall that one of the complaints against the *ancien régime* in France offered by the people who favored the Republic was that under the old regime some at least of the nobility had the right to insist that their peasants stay up all night in order to prevent the croaking of frogs from disturbing the sleep of their masters. I doubt this privilege was ever actually used, but complaints about it were used as propa-ganda for the Revolution. Which was the externality? This unused and obviously silly requirement or the use of it to over-throw the government?

The reader will no doubt feel that this is not a serious ques-tion. I agree. My point in bringing it up is that we do not have any way of telling externalities from other things, which either injure or benefit us. When I was in the infantry I frequently disliked various things, which were done to me and the other draftees. A 20-mile hike with full pack, gun and ammunition is something I would never have done voluntarily. Was this an externality? I think the standard answer to the question is 'no', but giving reasons for that is a little difficult. Arguing that it was not an externality because I was a citizen of the United States seems difficult.

Let us now discuss public goods. These are a special type of externality in which the benefit is widely dispersed. The subject was first discussed by Adam Smith[5] who pointed out that building bridges was beyond the funding capacity of individuals or companies and hence they should be built by the government. Today of course although we are accustomed to bridges being built by governments, we know that private companies can and sometimes do produce such public works. Toll bridges, toll roads, and such works as the Suez Canal have been built privately. Nevertheless, there are some things, which are hard to leave to the market. They are cases where it would be hard to coordinate the activities of a large number of totally unconnected enterprises. Altogether the conclusion I come to here is that we do not have a real definition of externality. We can easily make up a list of things, which government does and which, at one time or another, have been justified as reducing an externality. The problem with lists of this sort is that although we can agree on what the action of government was, we cannot agree on its desirability in every case.

The initial argument found in many economics textbooks until recently was that since many different individuals were using such facilities, say a bridge, it would not be possible to depend on them to build it. Harold Demsetz (1967), apparently having read Adam Smith, pointed out that if many different individuals are using a given facility, it is possible for a charge for each use to be imposed, but some other standard government activities such as military operations can hardly be paid for in this way. Thus a government agency with tax power is necessary. To call these public goods, however, seems a misnomer. That is particularly so since the words are also used for things like bridges. Nevertheless, that is the standard verbiage and I will continue to use it here. A special case is where more than one facility would be very inconvenient. We do not want a series of private companies tearing up our streets to build competing sewers. They can be and frequently are, produced by private companies but each company has a monopoly of the right to tear up a given street. There is no reason to believe that a government granted monopoly in this area is an optional system except for the difficulty of thinking of alternatives other than government direct provision.

To repeat, government action itself may be an externality and the only justification for the use of government in these cases rather than a bargain, is convenience. I am sure the reader, like myself, has a list of things where he would like a government to take action in order to abate an externality. If he has thought of the matter, he could also make a list of things which the government does and which affects him and which he dislikes. As far as I can see the actual allocation of government activity in this area is largely a matter of custom and convenience rather than a more carefully justified act. Only the government may use or threaten to use force in these areas. But what areas? Thus I end this chapter by confessing ignorance. If readers can clear up the problem I would greatly appreciate their thoughts.

Notes

1. *Washington Post*, 1 August 2004, p.A6.
2. A few western states permitted female voting in state elections before the extension of the franchise to all women in the United States.
3. Leaving Switzerland and Iceland out.
4. Gibbon's, *The Decline and Fall of the Roman Empire*, has been reprinted many times since it was first written in the eighteenth century.
5. Adam Smith, *The Wealth of Nations*, 1776. It is still in print with many publishers.

4. The poor

Long ago, when I was younger and just entering academe, the Earhart Foundation held a series of small conferences in which leading scholars in what was then called 'conservative' economics or political science gave lectures to younger people like myself. In those far distant days we 'conservatives' were thin on the ground. Academe was thoroughly dominated by what then and now are called 'liberals' in the United States. Thus these conferences had two effects: they provided a great improvement in the intellectual content of the conservative movement, particularly for the younger scholars, and in addition made clear that we were not entirely alone in the academic community as a whole, even if we were pretty much confined to the company of a few older scholars in our immediate universities.

The first such conference that I attended had three speakers one of whom was Milton Friedman. Among the many things that he talked about was charitable distribution and in particular the government's role. This was rather unpopular among the 'conservative' scholars attending the conference. In general they did not like income redistribution and as it happened the United States was quite prosperous at the time so the poor were not currently a major problem. His argument however, which so far as I know had never appeared anywhere before, was that the poor generated an externality by making the non-poor unhappy. If my recollection is right he asked us if we would be happy to see somebody starve to death in front of our house.

This was a difficult question for these anti-New Deal scholars and there was considerable complaint among the students. Some of them actually said that they would not do anything and would let the person starve. I am sure this is not what they would have done, but obviously we were thrown aback by the question.

In my case I agreed that something should be done but was not at all sure what. My eventual conclusion, and one which is important for this book, is that poverty and suffering do create an externality and hence call for at least some government action. What that action should be is the subject of this chapter.

Among the scholars I was perhaps the one who found this argument of Friedman's most compelling. In the earlier part of my life when I was in the diplomatic service I had been in China during and immediately after the Civil War and then in Korea at the last part of that war and the period immediately following. In both of these cases I had seen very genuine suffering and I assure you it inflicted pain on me. This was clearly an externality. Further, there was little I as a person could do about it. The problem was in both cases so great that an individual contributing as much as he could would not make a dent in it. I should say that with time you developed a sort of casual indifference to the problem. Particular cases would attract your attention, but not the general poverty we saw on the streets.

Let me give two specific examples. The old regime in China was dead when I arrived but there were remnants of it still around. Professional beggars, frequently severely mutilated, would ask for money. In some cases their parents, professional beggars, had mutilated them as children in order to make it more likely that they would attract sympathy and money. Placing a hot coal in the eye of the baby and hence permanently blinding it, or cutting the legs off so that the child as an adult would have to use his arms to get around, not only injured the child, but inflicted a serious externality on others including myself. We should remember that the parents who did this were in fact trying to benefit the child by giving him an asset that would provide income in later life. It was an example of the abject poverty in which most of the human race lived before about 1800 and in which much of it still lives, particularly in Africa. Of course, there were other beggars who had not been mutilated and there were many people who were not beggars, but who worked very, very, hard for a miserable life.

In Korea, the old regime had been eliminated in 1907 so that the particularly distressing cases I saw in China were not present. Bitter poverty was nevertheless common and this among people who not too long ago had had a living standard, which was way below America but still better than China by a good margin. Still poverty was painful from the standpoint of an America resident. To take but one example, the American Embassy was occupying a former Japanese business building. Next door there had been a house, but in the fighting it had burned down. All that was left was the brick fireplace and a chimney. This house and the yard in front of it was the sole residence of a gang of high-school age or younger boys. I don't know exactly how they made a living, probably picking up casual labor, but they certainly did not get enough to pay the rent on suitable housing. At night they clustered around the fireplace with as many as possible actually getting inside the fireplace for shelter. Fortunately when I saw them it was not winter so they did not freeze to death, but I would imagine a number of them were at least mildly ill. They built little bonfires in the front yard using scraps that they picked up and over this they cooked what I imagine were very poor meals. To say that they generated a negative externality on me is not only true, but I also felt unhappy that their mere presence created unhappy feelings in me. I had in essence a double externality, which sounds callous. Nevertheless it was a correct statement of my feelings.[1] I should say that most of us wealthy Americans, as time went by, gradually developed a feeling of annoyance and irritation when we saw these poor people. Further, at least in my case, I felt guilty about that annoyance. Thus in a way I had another externality inflicted on me by the poor. I should say that I do not think any of you will be sympathetic with me indeed I'm not sympathetic myself, and as I said above, I felt guilty about my own feelings.

There was no prospect of my making any significant dent in the problem by personal charity and indeed to make a gift to the beggars was positively dangerous. The fact that you were charitable would get around and you would find yourself continuously having to fight off further beggars. There were of course collective organizations, particularly connected with the Christian Church, that would take your money and spend it on the poor. Further there were a number of places in which the American troops who also saw the poverty, and wanted to help were making constructive contributions. The engineers in particular were equipped and trained to repair things like roads and many other regular units were able to engage in simple carpentry. Most of the Korean schools that I saw had a number of wooden swings, slides, and other playground equipment that had been made by the troops. Unfortunately the wood was not of too good quality and with time these deteriorated. Nevertheless it showed a charitable attitude, on the part of the soldiers. They too felt the externality.

Thus Milton Friedman was right in this as in so many other things. Open poverty generates an externality on the non-poor. Further, even when the poverty is not very open if we know it exists, we feel an externality and are likely to take action either to remedy the poverty or to remove it from our consciousness by any number of methods. I have noticed that, among my more liberal and 'bleeding hearts' acquaintances, there is a distinct reluctance to talk about the bitter poverty that one finds in such places as the Congo. Myself, I feel that a mother in the Sahel whose child is dying of malnutrition deserves much more aid than a black in one of our ghettos who does not have middle-class conveniences. It must be said however that the professional dispensers of aid in our government are more likely to help the second than the first.

As a matter of history, almost all governments have engaged in some kind of charitable behavior for the poor. In some cases this is shifted to a religion or an organized church, but normally the church receives some governmental support. The explanations for this are normally ethical but sympathy for the poor, particularly if they are obviously suffering is also usually an aspect. The pain inflicted by the suffering of the poor is an externality and I suppose the religious sanctions are also to be called externalities. If I believe that I face the prospect of an indefinite stay in hell if I do not perform my religious duty of charity, I am clearly suffering an externality inflicted by the existence of the poor.

Although almost all governments have taken steps to aid the poor and suffering, even if the steps may be very minor, it cannot be said that there is no waste in the process. One of the reasons for working is a desire not to starve to death. If some income is guaranteed, then people may be less motivated to engage in productive activity. Further the tax cost of this guarantee may reduce the incentives for other people to continue working, or in any event working hard. In a way both poverty and the means taken to help the poor create externalities and the problem is how to balance these externalities. I cannot say that historically, many governments have been very successful in this endeavor and, as the reader will shortly discover, I don't have any very conclusive solution to the problem myself.

In general, charity would lead one to be generous in dealing with those less fortunate than ourselves. There are limitations of course. Only saints give away enough to inflict a real deprivation on themselves. Still, all of us to some extent do reduce our living standards if measured by direct consumption and if we do not include the satisfaction derived by gifts to people or organizations that we think deserve support. There is a whole industry devoted to soliciting and expending money. But partly this is a church activity and most religions have offered at least some compensation for payments to them. The protection from the pains of hell or more crudely specific benefits in this world is often part of the 'sales package' offered by these religious institutions as part of their solicitation of funds.

In many cases, however, there is no such countervailing promise to the simple donor. But there are more complex examples. I expect that the reader is, as I am, bombarded by mailed solicitations for various good causes. I even get telephone calls. I presume that the reader, like myself again, normally does not generously fulfill the needs of these soliciting organizations, but does occasionally provide funds. In this case it is not obvious whether the externality is the suffering, which those doing the soliciting allege they will relieve, or the inconvenience, which the solicitation imposes on its recipient. Presumably both should be counted. It may be that the suffering of the ultimate recipient by causing the organization of these soliciting outfits, generates an additional externality.

Until the Great Depression, the poor in the United States were dealt with by the county governments. This implies that charitable impulses make even small democracies help the poor. Liebergott (1976) collected data shown in Table 4.1 on payments that were made. The arrangement guaranteed income to anyone. The income was not generous. It amounted to about a quarter of the wage of common labor. This means of course that it was different in different counties, but would prevent severe deprivation. With the Great Depression, the program was taken over by the federal government and it's not obvious whether this meant that the poor were benefited or injured. So far as I know no statistician has attempted to extend Liebergott's series to the present and I would suggest this as an excellent project for a graduate student looking for a good doctoral dissertation.

Table 4.1   Poor relief

	As percentage of the earnings of common labor
1850	22
1860	26
1870	24
1903	23
1929	31
1940	28
1950	29
1960	28
1970	29

In addition to straightforward efforts to raise living standards of the poor we engage in other activity, which is intended to benefit people other than our immediate family. Missionary activity is a particular case. We usually think of missionary activity in connection with Christianity but a lot of other religions engage in it too. Both Moslems and Hindus maintain missions in the United States for the purpose of converting people to their religion. In both cases they are fairly small and in both cases, like Christian missionaries in non-Christian areas, there is an existing small church of believers and the missionaries deal with them also. Clearly people who make gifts for the missionary activity are attempting to benefit others and, of course, sacrificing to some extent for that purpose. Thus you might say that a Moslem going on pilgrimage to Mecca exerts an externality on Christians in Peoria. It's not clear whether this externality should be measured by the amount the Christian contributes to his church for missionary activity, or an additional negative externality from the mere knowledge that there are other believers.

There are other cases in which activity creates negative externalities upon people who wish to benefit the actor and think that the activity injures him. An obvious case is laws against drug addiction. People who favor these laws feel the drug addiction injures the addict and wish to benefit him by curing him of this addiction. Currently most intellectuals tend to be opposed to restrictions on drugs particularly marijuana. Before going on to discuss this I should reveal my own position. While I was studying at the University of Chicago in the 1930s I decided that the laws should be repealed. I had not and have not since taken any drug except alcohol. I did not drink alcohol until I joined the diplomatic service where it was a social requirement. I continued mild social drinking after I left and today I drink one glass every day for the benefit of my heart. I have never smoked.

It is frequently said that it is impossible to prevent consumption of such drugs as opium and its derivatives. History indicates that it is not impossible because in the 1930s there was very little consumption of such drugs in either the UK or the United States. They used different methods than we do today, and it might be difficult to switch to these methods now.

Starting with the UK, a person who was addicted to one of these drugs could go to a doctor and get a certificate of addiction, which made it possible for him to buy drugs at the regular drugstore. They were cheaper and of better quality than smuggled equivalents. It was easy to find a shady doctor who would be willing to give a regular prescription for such things because the addict was a low-cost high-pay patient. Unfortunately the current government-provided medical system in the UK has changed this. Today the doctor does not bill his patient for every treatment, but puts the patient on a list and is paid annually for each patient he has. Thus the dope addict with his frequent calls for a prescription, is now an unprofitable patient and doctors now make efforts to cure them of their addiction by cutting down the dose. This has made it possible for an illegal drug industry to develop although it is much less developed than that in the United States.

In the United States in the 1930s not only was sale of the drugs illegal, but consumption of them was also. The federal government maintained two prisons, called hospitals, where someone who was addicted would be shut up and cured by gradually reducing his dose. This is a tedious and very unpleasant process. When the man was cured and released he would have lost all his contacts and would be watched carefully by the police. As a result the cure was frequently permanent.

Both of these methods worked well when the total number of addicts was low. With millions of addicts they would be hard to implement. We mainly today try to cut off supplies, which is a most difficult process. The fact that there is a very substantial intellectual community, which objects to these laws even though most of them do not personally take drugs, makes them more difficult to cut off. In general we have turned to a very inept foreign policy in which we try to get other countries not to produce the drugs rather than preventing their transportation to and sale in the United States. I have no suggestions for those people who honestly think that drug addiction is not only a sin but also a disease. Since I am a moral relativist, I cannot criticize their position except to point out that it is very difficult to implement.

There are other areas where people wish to control the behavior of other people for ethical reasons. As a particularly obvious example, consider sexual matters. To take one example, prostitution is at least formally illegal although normally we make no great efforts to enforce those laws. When I was young, homosexuality was about as wicked a thing as you could do, but now it's regarded as mildly noble. For another case, abortion was an extremely serious crime both in law and in ethics in those dear dead days[2] but today is apparently regarded as positively virtuous. Alcohol consumption is banned by some religions, and, of course, drinking while driving is thought to be a very serious offense.

In all of these cases, certain types of activity generate negative externalities with a result that actions are undertaken to reduce or eliminate this behavior. Of course the actions taken to restrict it generate externalities upon the people who want to continue consuming opium or hiring prostitutes. If some people in the society feel sorry for the poor and wish to have a government tax-financed program to deal with them this exerts externalities on those who do not want to pay the taxes. The mere physical presence of the poor may generate externalities as I have emphasized above. The mere physical existence of the Internal Revenue Service may also create externalities on the people who object to this use of the taxes.

In usual parlance, payment of money to the poor is called income redistribution and is motivated by desire to eliminate the externality which the poor create. Preventing people from buying drugs, consorting with prostitutes, and engaging in various other activities, which are objected to because they are thought to injure the persons in question also involves reducing externalities. In some cases these externalities come from the fact that the acting person injures himself and hence makes the well-intentioned bystander feel some pain. In other cases the activity actually injures people other then the actors. My trumpet playing in the first chapter is an example, as is drunken driving. In general however the elimination of such activities is not really considered income redistribution even though they lead to the actor being worse off and the interested bystander feeling happier.

Notes

1. If the reader would like to get a good idea of the reality of poverty in the backward part of the world William Easterly has written a book, *The Elusive Quest for Growth* (2002). Most it is a description of efforts to promote growth, but he interrupts his discussion of this frequently for actual description of terrible poverty in the poorer parts of the world.
2. Infanticide was common in China when I was first there, but nominally illegal. In the United States it is illegal and considered wicked.

5.　The legacy of Bismarck

The modern state is largely a mechanism for transferring funds from one person to another. What we economists call public goods are provided by the state but are now only a part of it. The United States is not as far along in this procedure as many other countries, but in our case the federal government pays out in various types of transfers a significant percent of the amount it collects in taxes. Most of the European countries are even more dominated by the legacy of Bismarck.

The reason I refer to this as his legacy is because he invented the modern Social Security system. Charitable payments by the state have of course a long history, but the particular system we now use was introduced by Bismarck. It is ironic that he introduced it in an effort to defeat the socialists in an election. It failed. Today the elaborate social security system is almost the definition of socialism since direct government management of the economy is currently very unfashionable and either gone or being slowly eliminated wherever it previously existed. I would like to think that this is a permanent situation since the Bismarckian income transfer system does not necessarily greatly injure the economy in the way a planned economy would. Unfortunately, prediction is difficult and in addition the Bismarckian system does injure the economy but not in the same way.

The activities of the Bismarckian welfare state can be roughly divided into three categories. The first and in some ways most important, is attention to people who are old. The exact definition of it varies from nation to nation. In the United States the pensions begin for most people at 65. People not in good health may get disability pensions earlier. The second category is state medical attention for at least some people. In many countries it is universal, but in the United States it starts at 65 although poor people get state medical attention earlier. The third part is aid to the unemployed. Traditional charity was widespread before Bismarck introduced the welfare state. In many cases of course it was private or church aid not government, but governments were deeply involved in many countries.

Bismarck regularized it and changed the method of payment. Further, in essence he increased the payments to the old, although since the previous payments were rather irregular, not everyone received larger payments. Since almost everyone also paid, the advantage to recipients was not obvious. In order to explain the system easily, we may concentrate on discussing the old age pension system. Before Bismarck, older people were dependent in part on their savings, in part on their younger relatives, and in part on payments by charitable organizations one of which was usually the state. Bismarck did not make the first two of these items illegal but he reformed the government share in order to make it more regular.

Basically, and remember we are talking about aid to the old only at this point, all workers were taxed with the tax depending on their wage. Bismarck was a brilliant politician and the system was nominally paid in part by the worker by a reduction in his wage and partially by the employer who paid a tax on the money that he paid to the worker as a salary. Of course the entire amount was paid by the worker whose salary was reduced by the amount of the tax paid by the employer. Bismarck was however, as I said above, a brilliant politician and he thought that the workers would not figure this out. He turned out to be right and most of them think they're getting a bargain because the amount shown on their payment certificate is only half of the actual cost. The proposal of the Clinton family to provide medical attention under somewhat similar circumstances went Bismarck one better. Only 20 percent of the cost was to be directly subtracted from the workers pay with the other 80 percent coming from the employer and, of course, reducing the wage he nominally paid the worker. The program failed politically but as far as I can see almost nobody saw through the subterfuge. Certainly the newspapers I read did not realize the whole cost would be borne by the worker.

When the worker reaches the magic age, 65 in the United States, he begins receiving a pension. Originally there were various procedures to make certain he stopped working. In the United States originally a dollar was taken off his pension for each dollar he earned before the age of 72. In recent years this amount was reduced and now has been abolished. Thus a person over the age of 65 may be doing very well financially if he has the kind of job an older person can successfully carry out and also has the pension. It is not obvious however that someone who went into the program when he first started working and then began drawing the pension at 65 has done well. If he had invested the same amount, the income he began getting at 65 together with the sizable capital amount he holds would probably make him better off. Of course that assumes that the money was invested wisely, when talking about private investment, and that the government did not collapse into inflation if we are talking about the government pension scheme. It is unclear which of the two 'investments' is best and I think that the fraud in pretending that the worker pays less than he actually does may be the reason for the popularity of the state pension.

There is however another difference between this program and a private saving program. Suppose Bismarck had proposed that all workers take the same amount as a total tax, worker and employers share, and invest it in an insurance policy. The insurance company would invest it in some kind of securities and we shall assume that the investment is successful. Further in calculating the pension that they would pay they would make actuarial calculations as to the time people would die. Thus people who died quickly would be in essence making payments to those who died later. This is different from personal savings where there is no transfer from the people who suffer early deaths to those who live longer.

Assuming that we feel that insurance companies are as trust-worthy as the state, the scheme seems to be a better old age pension than the previous system. Bismarck's modern followers, however, did not require people to save money to get a pension. When the system was first set up in the United States it did involve the payments being saved and then paid out when the pensioner reached the age of 65. That was quickly changed, however. From 1940 until a few years ago the payments of the young employed persons were promptly paid out to the pensioners. Only a small amount was set aside for contingencies. When the system was first set up to those who were old enough to be pensionable, since they had paid little or no taxes, made a large profit. The younger people who paid for this profit did not do so well, although they may not have made any real serious loss. In general the older you were when the system was introduced the more advantageous it was for you.

An aspect of the scheme that has attracted a good deal of attention recently is that individuals paying into the system make their payments long before they draw their pension. Thus one would think that the lack of interest payments on these early contributions meant that they do not do very well. In practice however, with rising living standards, Congress from time to time increases the pension. This does not do as well for the pensioners as they would have received an interest payment and then had their payments increased because other people died early, but they have not done very badly. Presumably Congress will keep this policy up and eventually if the scheme continues, the pensioners will do reasonably well.

Looking at the scheme in general it involves an odd redistribution along the lifespan of the participants. They pay when they are young and then receive payments when they retire. Further, as a result of very recent modifications, they do not have to retire in order to get the payments. All I have to do is get older. But this is people who come into the system when it is mature. When it was first inaugurated people who were relatively elderly did very well and the younger people nearly broke even. The political advantages of such a scheme are obvious, and it is not surprising that a very intelligent politician (President Roosevelt) inaugurated it.

But what happens if the scheme is dropped. The USSR had

a system of old age pensions, which also redistributed from the young to the old and when the USSR collapsed, great hardships were imposed on the elderly. Recent Russian proposals to change the system by permitting private investment have been criticized on the grounds that a private investment might not work out well. This is quite true, but it should be pointed out that governments are not really 100 percent reliable. Financial problems leading to inflation may result in significant losses by the holders of this kind of pension. If the system is stopped or inflated out the older people will do very badly. Whether this is likely or not I leave to the reader. The great gains made by the older people at the beginning might be counterbalanced by great losses made by people who were younger when they entered the system and do not receive their pensions.

Bismarck also provided a medical scheme that provided fees for hospitals and doctors. Note when he first inaugurated the system it may have had perverse effects on health. Theories and knowledge of the place of germs in causing disease was only just beginning at that time and hospitals and doctors were not particularly sanitary. At least one kind of disease, childbirth fever, was discovered to be transmitted by doctors. Thus the medical program may, in its first years, have actually increased the death rate. In the long run of course, as doctors and hospitals took up extreme sanitation and special drugs were invented to cure diseases, it had a significant positive effect on life expectancy.

Note however that the increase in life expectancy came because some people who otherwise would not have obtained hospital or medical attention because of poverty now did so. In England, as a peculiar special effect, the death rate of the poor actually increased in the first few years of the National Health Service. Before its establishment, two groups of people received very good medical attention in England. The wealthy, of course, had enough money to get very good medical service. The government provided excellent medical attention for the poor. The people between those two classes found it necessary, at least to some extent, to economize on their medical treatment. When the system was converted to a universal system, this meant that a good many medical services were provided for the middle income group for free, and they increase their consumption. This led to a significant, but obviously temporary, reduction in medical attention for the poor, with a concomint increase in the death rate (Tullock 1984).

Health provisions vary a good deal from country to country. That it leads to better medical attention for the poor is in most cases clear. The attention however is not so good that people who have large private resources are likely to use it instead of private physicians.

Instead of attempting to describe the system everywhere, let me turn to the United States. The system here is peculiar and an outlier among government sponsored health situations. First, there are separate medical attention systems for military people and retired military people. Further federal government employees have another separate system. Leaving the special systems aside, we have a paid medical insurance program for older people and a separate one for people who have been formally classified as impoverished. The rest of the people are urged to buy private insurance but not required to do so.

Private health insurance was invented in the United States in the 1930s. When World War II was being financed by inflation the government wished to conceal the inflation by enacting a set of price and wage controls. The labor unions and the private employers who found it difficult to hire enough employees without raising wages reached a compromise under which companies bought health insurance for their workers and the federal government did not include the cost in the worker's salary for income tax purposes. The system was retained after the war with the result that if your employer gave you health insurance this was quite a sizable supplement to your income. A similar cash increase in pay would have been taxed and thus the employer would have to give you more than the price of the insurance to raise your income to the same extent. The situation is bizarre but Congress has shown reluctance to change it.

Purchasing your own health insurance normally requires a physical examination and sometimes the company will refuse to insure you or quotes you a rate which takes into account some pre-existing condition. This, of course, increases the cost of the insurance and the fact that the state governments have enacted a number of minor laws prohibiting companies from raising insurance fees in consequence of some types of health effects means that private insurance is usually not a good bargain, particularly for young people in good health. Thus people tend to seek employment from companies that provide health insurance for all employees. Rather bizarrely they are not subject to the same problems because they purchase a health insurance program for a large collection of people and the insurance company actuarially assumes it is just like any other large group of people. Small companies with 10 or less employees are normally not given treatment similar to that of the large companies and hence health insurance is not a bargain for them either. The result of all this is that many people either do not have health insurance or feel that they are paying an excessive price for it.

All this is supplemented however by a bizarre system in which if you are ill or injured, you have a right to treatment in the emergency room of any hospital that maintains one. The hospital will make efforts to collect payment from you, but for the poor these efforts rarely lead to anything. The hospital will thus have to raise its rates on paying patients with the result that the regular fees are increased. This makes it even less of a bargain to buy individual health insurance than it would be without this special additional factor. I should emphasize that Bismarck did not invent this. Stan Laurel and Oliver Hardy also had nothing to do with it.

6. Some biological problems

The reader has no doubt so far felt more or less at home with the previous chapters since they deal with behavior, which is not too far distant from his own. He no doubt makes contributions to charities, may contribute to the church, and occasionally feels called upon to contribute to a fund to assist people in some distant disaster. If there is an earthquake in Turkey, a flood in Venezuela, or famine in Ethiopia, many Americans certainly including at least some of the readers of this book, will make voluntary contributions to the victims. There are indeed special organizations that do nothing except solicit such donations and then expend them, wisely, we hope.

The reader also no doubt believes in the theory of evolution. Even most churchgoers accept the general process of natural selection. I doubt the reader who has read thus far realizes that there is an apparent and obvious contradiction between these two parts of his psyche. Evolution selects not for niceness, but for producing the maximum number of descendants. If you make a contribution instead of spending the money to improve the education or health of your son, daughter, or grandchildren you reduce the likely number of your descendants. Natural selection should, over time, eliminate your particular family in favor of a more selfish, family-oriented, hereditary line.

Since the reader no doubt makes contributions to various charities and favors his government taxing him for other charitable payments not to his children, he may be puzzled by the above reasoning. I know that when I talk about it to colleagues even or, especially, those with economic training, they are always convinced that there is something wrong with my reasoning. They point out that they enjoy making these contributions and when I say that if their inherited preference function leads them to enjoy such contributions, one would think that their hereditary line would have no great prospects for the future, they offer various rationalizations for their behavior. Further their contributions to people far away tend to be quite small. They do spend more for the education of their children than for the education of the children of Africans.

The experience in talking with people about this matter seems to show that it is very difficult to convince them that there is a theoretical contradiction here. They feel a sense of satisfaction when making charitable contributions. As a general rule evolution has designed us so that we like things that are good for us. Hume said that the great governors of our behavior were pleasure and pain. We take action intended to gain pleasure and avoid things, which were painful. Hume did not know about evolution, but may have thought that there was some conscious design here. He was of course an atheist and hence may have felt that it is just accident that our preferences are for things that are good for us. In any event, however, he and his good friend Adam Smith thought that following our preferences is usually good for us and no doubt would have extended it to the statement that it is good for our descendants too.

I find, in talking to modern people who believe in evolution, that the view that making charitable contributions does, to a certain extent, have survival value is widespread. To some degree this is simply a generalization of the proposition that things that we want to do are good for us. We like sweet foods and the biologists will tell us that in previous times food with high sugar content was highly nutritious and hence we were selected to seek it out. Now, of course, most citizens of the United States or Europe do not need such concentrated food and health advisors tell us that we should be careful with it. But it takes many generations for evolution to adjust to changes in the environment and hence we still like sweet foods. If sweet foods were really bad for us under present conditions we would probably adjust rather quickly, but as a matter of fact in moderation they do no real harm provided we keep our teeth cleaned.

The general proposition that things we like to do are good for us and are likely to provide more descendants along our gene line is correct. Since we do enjoy making charitable contributions in moderation it is not unreasonable to feel that this also will lead to more descendants. It could be reasoned, that keeping good relations with other members of the group would have survival value. Clearly this would not however lead to our making gifts to the victims of a flood in Venezuela. Even there, however, it could be argued that making the gifts indicate to the people with whom we have many contacts that we are 'good people'.

The same argument looks better when we are directly dealing with people with whom we have regular contacts. Being nice and generous to friends and acquaintances might lead them to be nice and generous to us and our children and hence increase the number of descendants. It may also mean that we have less in the way of friction in our regular dealings and hence, once again, a higher survival value of ourselves and for our descendants. Unfortunately both of these two arguments fail if we think about them carefully.

Suppose we make gifts to other members of our group and they make gifts back. If we could make gifts just a little bit smaller than they do, we would gain and have more descendants. There should then be a sort of contest in which each individual or gene line attempts to give a little less than it gets. Over time this would lead to a gradual reduction in gifts and eventually none. If we look at our close relatives, the chimpanzees, we observe this line of reasoning more or less completed. They make very few gifts to other than their direct and known descendants.[1] Chimpanzees occasionally kill monkeys and eat them. The chimpanzee with some meat may well make a gift of it to friends and acquaintances. This does not apply to fruit or nuts, which are simply eaten. Primitive human beings make somewhat the same distinction. The hunter may well share the deer or whatever he has killed with other members of his tribe. He will rarely directly share other kinds of food.

There is one obvious explanation for this differentiation.

Meat is normally acquired in a quantity large enough so that it cannot be eaten all at once by one person. Meat, however tends to spoil and become dangerous very quickly. A chimpanzee or any Stone Age human being who hoarded meat for his own or his family's consumption, would run very large risks of dying of various food poisons. Hence giving it away in hopes that there will be eventual reciprocation could well be evolutionarily selected because of the danger. This would not apply to fruit, nuts, or other vegetable food, which make up the bulk of the diet of chimpanzees. Primitive humans also got the bulk of their diet from the gathering carried on by the females rather than hunting carried on by males.

I may not have convinced you that charitable activity outside the immediate family should be selected out by evolution. We will return to this topic after a few paragraphs. First, however, may I explain the perfectly good biological reasons, which might lead to specific charitable activity. My argument will be based on Dawkins' book *The Selfish Gene* (1989), and more specifically on an article by myself (2002).

Basically the mechanism of inheritance is by gene transmission with the animals, plants, etc. merely acting as host for successive generations of genes. Thus if a gene caused its host to take action which benefited another animal, plant, etc. containing the same gene, there will be more copies of that gene in the next generation. Thus to say that the gene protects its duplicates in other hosts is not exactly accurate but does convey the general meaning.

There is a famous statement made in a bar in the course of an informal conversation, by a prominent biologist, that he would take a 50-percent chance of sacrificing his own life to save a brother and a one-in-four chance of sacrificing his life to save a cousin. The statement is frequently repeated by biologists but there is no original citation because of the informal way in which he made the remark. In fact, of course, he would require slightly more than 50 percent and slightly more than one in four, but this is the correct calculation for a gene to make if genes were able to calculate. Although they cannot calculate they may be able to instruct their hosts to take action along these lines. Of course the sacrifice for direct descendants would be larger if you knew who they were. The female knows which are her children but the males can never be sure. Still within the tribe the chances of legitimacy are fairly good among humans who have more or less permanent mating arrangements. Among chimpanzees the chances are very much worse.

Thus we have reasons for believing that adults will make some sacrifice for what appear to be their descendants. They should also make sacrifices for cousins and their descendants in those cases, as among human beings, in which there are groups of people or animals larger than a simple breeding pair and members of the groups are at least distantly related. We can assume that human beings driven by their genes will be charitable towards relatives with the degree of charity falling off as they become more and more distantly related. This, of course, is what we observe among human beings. So far as I know, a similar charity gradient has not been observed among the other primates. I do not think we need concern ourselves very much about this apparent difference between our closest non-human relatives and ourselves.

We must now turn to another aspect of heredity. Interbreeding among close relatives is very dangerous because it tends to preserve bad genes. Many of those animals that live in fairly large groups normally, have some mechanism to avoid interbreeding. All the males, for example, when they reach adulthood either leave or are driven out of the group. They seek mates in other tribes, which have a similar custom, and thus provide a vacancy. With chimpanzees, oddly it is the females who leave.

We do not really have a lot of information about human beings who live in primitive tribal societies. Many of them certainly have arrangements for trading mates between different sub-tribes. There may, for example, be an annual meeting in which a group of bands get together. I do not know of any careful study of this example and its effects on mating, but it certainly would fit well with a tribal out-breeding custom. If we turn to more civilized groups, for example England before the Industrial Revolution, the bulk of the population lived in small villages and it is my impression, admittedly not the result of serious research by myself or anyone else, that they practiced the same kind of exogamy. Perhaps not perfectly, as the village idiot is a standard literary figure, which may imply that they did engage in inbreeding and hence had occasional bad gene connections.

Large cities like London did not of course have this custom. But until well into the Industrial Revolution such large cities were deathtraps. They far from replaced their own population because of deaths from disease. They lived on continuous immigration from the villages. Even in the United States in which the population was much less dense and hence cities less crowded, death rates in cities were higher than in the villages. So far as I know there are no studies of the marital customs, which would show whether country villages tend to outbreed or inbreed. It seems unlikely however that there was a large amount of inbreeding in most areas. Once again turning to a literature theme, mountain villages in the South, which were rather isolated, are frequently portrayed as having mental defectives.

Then what does all this have to do with charity to China? At first glance not much, but if we consider the genes they may explain it. First a gene does not think, but it does control to some extent the brains of thinking entities. The obvious example of this is sexual attraction, which we find in many animals with brains in all sizes. The human being and the butterfly are examples. But sexual attraction is not the only thing in which the brain is controlled by genes. I am about to argue that our charitable impulses, from giving things to your children, to making charitable contributions for missionaries attempting to convert the heathen, are influenced by the genes.

Naturally the genes do not make careful calculations, but they do have influence. Let me go back to the biologist who said that he would run a risk of (slightly less than) 50 percent death to save a brother from certain death. His direct descendants will be reduced by such an act. Thus the number of most of his genes will be reduced in the next generation to less than they would have been had he not engaged in this self-sacrifice. The number of the particular gene which pushed him into engaging in the act however has been somewhat increased over what it would have been had he followed a simple self-serving policy. In a way this particular gene is at war with the other genes that he carries. One would anticipate that there might be some kind of protection against such genes in the rest of the gene train, but as far as I know this matter has not been investigated. It would in any event, be hard to research.

This however simply tells you that your genes will instruct you to make some sacrifice for close relatives. How about more distant relatives? The gene, which told you to take a 50 percent chance of death to save a second cousin, would be eliminated from the population fairly quickly. On the other hand as a biologist would say, 'A one in four chance of death to save a cousin would pay for the particular gene'. Of course most animals and for that matter most human beings do not have very accurate knowledge of distant relatives and hence their genes could hardly be instructed in the relationship and hence 'decide' for whom they should sacrifice.

But this deals with relatives, not complete strangers living in China. How do we account for people making some sacrifice motivated by the likelihood that the gene pool that they have will be perpetuated in order to benefit a stranger in China? In order to answer this question we have to turn back some way and consider when human beings lived in small bands with only casual contact between the bands. And here we return to the fact that exogamy was necessary in order to avoid the dangers of incest and the perpetuation of dangerous genes.

Consider the inhabitants of a small tribe of humans (or chimpanzees) who practiced outbreeding. Let us assume that males always leave the tribe when they reach maturity. Normally they would join other nearby tribes but sometimes would go farther away. The result of this process is that an individual in the tribe will not only have some relationship to other members of the tribe, but also weaker relationships to the next tribe over. But these tribes also practice exogamy so the individual would have a reasonable chance, perhaps one in 32, of sharing a gene with someone in the next tribe over. This relationship would continue for a longer distance with steadily reducing amount of gene sharing.

But if we go back to the time when the human species was developing its present genetic constitution, the people simply did not know of the existence of tribes beyond the ones which were fairly close. Thus the genes might 'think' that all humans shared some of their genes for giving gifts, which will preserve genes in existence. Thus we would have a drive to give at least something to people suffering at great distance. Our knowledge of the relationship would gradually decline with distance. Naturally the genes don't think, but a gene, which acted in this way, would perpetuate, not itself, but its duplicates. Note that a gene that instructed its host to make a sacrifice for another entity which might have a duplicate of that gene would increase the total number of such genes in the population but reduce the likelihood that it itself will be present in the next generation. It will also reduce the likelihood that the other genes with which it shares the bearer will be present in the next generation. If such genes were frequent and powerful in a given species we could predict that the specie itself will cease to exist. Thus in order for the gene to perpetuate itself it has to avoid killing too many of its hosts. Since the human species does exist, our generosity genes must have avoided this trap.

All this looks very complicated, and is. It does however explain why we may make gifts to very, very distant people. To repeat what I said earlier, when I talk to people about the matter I normally find that they have great difficulty in recognizing the very existence of the problem. They, like myself, make such gifts and feel satisfaction when they do so.

Above I quoted David Hume on things that give us satisfaction being good for us. I seem to have turned up a case where that is not true. Further most of the people that I discuss the matter with take the view that it's a much simpler matter since they enjoy these gifts. They have never normally even thought about the evolutionary significance of them. In many cases they seem to feel that the mere feeling of satisfaction that they get from the gift is proof that it is desirable not only to the recipient but to the giver.

When they reach this point in the discussion, they normally say that these gifts are beneficial to the giver because he may receive reciprocal gifts which will more then repay the original gift. This would, of course, raise question of why the person reciprocating with more then he receives is not selected out by evolution. Once again I find that most people regard this question and problem as false. In all these cases someone gives away more than he receives. Darwinian selection, at its simplest, should eliminate this kind of thing, but it does not.

Another explanation that I sometimes encounter is simply that general relations are improved if people think you are generous. Thus the gift to the starving Chinese benefits you because people in your own circle in the United States regard this as something certifying you to have a good character and hence they treat you better than they otherwise would. I don't doubt that this kind of thing does happen, but remember you pay for it. Always giving a little bit less, but not enough less to be conspicuous would benefit you on both dimensions. Thus over generations we might find a steady continuous decline in such gifts with the ones who pay the lowest gifts producing more grandchildren. Once again, evolution would select against generosity.

To repeat what I've said above, all this implies that some of our most virtuous drives would tend to get us eliminated by evolution. My explanation is that the drive does indeed tend to reduce the number of descendants of its victim in the next generation, but increases the number of duplicates of the particular gene that causes it. This seems paradoxical, and I don't deny that it is, but it is a better explanation for charity to distant people than any other that I know. If readers have thought of a better one, I hope they will communicate it to me.

But to anticipate the next chapter, much of our charitable giving is done by way of the state. If we look at this part of our charitable giving we find quite large gifts to people within our national entity whenever it is, but the level of such gifts falls off abruptly at the national border. Instead of a gradual fall-off as you leave the individual or the national group there is a plateau followed by a cliff and then another plain at a much lower level. This is only an approximate fit to the theory given above, but it's unfortunately true that our theories are rarely in perfect accord with nature (Tullock 2002).

Note

1. They may engage in grooming on almost any other member of the band. Whether the main gainer is the subject of the grooming or the groomer who eats bugs and things derived in the grooming process is not clear. In any event, the cost is substantially nil.

7. The rich

The last three chapters dealt with the type of externalities that we feel when someone else is poverty-stricken or in pain or any kind of distress. It is certainly true that most people have this type of feeling and that they at least occasionally do something about it. In this chapter we will turn to the mirror image of this, the discomfort we may have when we feel when someone else has too much. I might, for example, feel you should give me some of your money.[1]

Transfers and aid within a society or between societies can be a consequence of both of these types of externalities although to some extent they tend to cancel each other out. I can be sincerely sorry for someone who is ill while at the same time feeling that it would be desirable that some of his wealth be transferred to me. If we look at existing governments we find that they engage in both types of transfers. In some cases they will aid the poor and in other cases milk the rich. Of course the money taken from the rich may be used to aid the poor. In both cases, we are dealing with an externality which depends upon the well-being of someone else.

Further, what we feel, and how strongly we feel it, may be deeply affected by connections or simple distance. I used to run an experiment when I was in Tucson, where most of the political science department were politically on the left and felt that we should help the poor. I used to annoy such people by pointing out that Tucson was only 100 miles from the Mexican border and that border is one of the places in the world where average income changes most abruptly. I would point out that if they wished to help the poor, the poor in Nogales were both poorer and closer than the poor in the ghettos of New York. To use an example which I inflicted on them, a poor woman in

Nogales who found feeding her children difficult attracted more of my sympathy than a poor person in New York who did not have a color television.

It was obvious that this question bothered them. Normally what they did was quickly to change the subject rather than trying to rationalize the fact that they favored a government program to give money to the poor woman without color TV, over helping the poor Mexican to feed her children. They would like to do both, but if economies were necessary, they would favor the black US citizen in New York.

Of course there are many people in the world who are much poorer than the Mexicans. Mexico in fact is probably about halfway up the ladder from poverty-stricken Congo to wealthy Switzerland. Thus if we were attempting to simply alleviate poverty we would not only fail to send any money to the ghettos of New York, we probably would also not send it to Mexico. This assumes, of course, some limitation on how much we can give. My leftist friends should have been in favor of world equalization of incomes, but they were not.[2] They did prefer that blacks living in New York have higher incomes than blacks living in the Congo although they had no rationale for this.

Rawls, in his famous book *Justice as Fairness* (2001), mainly avoids the problem. Behind his famous veil of ignorance you know what country you are a citizen of. The poorer parts of the world are dealt with only in a part of one paragraph where he says that if the poverty of a poor country is due to a shortage of natural resources perhaps we should help. I should say that this was necessary for the great popularity of his book. If he suggested actual egalitarianism over the world, which would have meant that his colleagues on the Harvard faculty would lose something like 80 percent of their income, he would have received an outburst of unfavorable reviews and criticism.

It is and was my opinion that Rawls and his favorable reviewers expressed normal human attitudes much better than I. A very brief inquiry among close acquaintances shows that is so. Of course my close acquaintances may be a very deviant sample. James Buchanan, my co-author of *The Calculus of*

Consent (1965), in conversation took a straightforward patriotic attitude saying that of course you help citizens as opposed to non-citizens. Some people told me that they would help people closer to them rather than farther away. Since the citizens of Nogales were closer to my friends in Tucson than people living in New York this did not rationalize their behavior, but they may have meant socially closer. In general they simply looked puzzled by the problem. In discussion with employees of the international aid organizations I find that normally they are genuinely very sorry for people who live in the countries in which they are distributing aid. On the other hand they live at a fairly high living standard, pay no taxes and rarely reduce their incomes significantly to help the poor. Since that was my attitude in China and Korea I understand this empathetically, but not intellectually.

This is merely a prologue for the latter part of this book. We do help the poor because their poverty inflicts externalities on us; but we also take money from other people because their prosperity inflicts externalities upon us. Whether taking money from other people who are wealthier than we are and spending it ourselves, is an externality is a matter of definition. Above, I mentioned James Buchanan and his attitude towards helping citizens as opposed to strangers or more accurately, citizens *more* than strangers. He also had a very strong positive dislike of inherited wealth. On one occasion he and I had a fairly long dispute on this issue (Tullock 1997). I sent an article on inherited wealth into one of the journals and it was published. I recommended that if inheritance is to be taxed, the tax should be not more than the amount which maximized government revenue. Buchanan not only disagreed with me, he was extremely vigorous in his disagreement. He actually favored totally abolishing inheritance of wealth. He did not write a criticism of my article but three of his graduate students, very likely inspired by him, wrote strongly negative comments on my article.

To repeat, my article recommended that inheritance taxes not be higher than those which brought in the largest revenue to the government. I did not actually recommend raising taxes to that point but my difference with Buchanan dealt with his desire to lower inherited wealth even if this led to lower tax revenue drawn from wealthy people. The phenomenon of a tax level that brings in the maximum revenue when higher taxes actually bring in less revenue is usually referred to as the 'Laffer curve', but in fact is much older than the Reagan Administration. Laffer, a high official in that Administration, in fact did not claim that he invented it, merely that he explained it to some other high officials in the government. The view that the Reagan tax cuts would lead to a higher level of prosperity and therefore to a higher tax income for the government is not part of the original Laffer curve line of reasoning although it was endorsed by many officials in the Reagan Administration. Laffer himself, at first did not push that line, but I believe that after a while he joined those officials of the Reagan Administration who did.

But regardless of this deviation into recent political history, there is no doubt that many people do feel a negative externality when someone else has more than they do. We can feel a negative externality from the prosperity of someone else, even if it is less than our own. Consider a feudal lord many centuries ago who discovers that a merchant in town is doing quite well even if he is nowhere near as wealthy as the lord. He may feel that commoners just should not have that much money, only the nobility. Most of us will regard this as an undesirable emotion, but we can understand it. Even more common is the envy we feel for people who have more money than we do. It is not only money, which can lead to this kind of negative externality. I may envy high-ranking academics, people who received the Medal of Honor, or the President of the United States. As a general rule, ethical leaders will argue that this kind of envy is undesirable. I do not deny that, but I do point out that it is quite common.

Confining ourselves to resenting people who have more money than we do, we observe that governments take action to reduce this kind of externality. At the moment of writing there is a considerable debate in Washington between those who want the top brackets of the income tax cut back and those who do not. Confining ourselves temporarily to the second group only, the externality they feel is compounded of two elements. One is a desire to actually spend the wealth of the upper income groups themselves and the other is a feeling that it is ideal to take it away just because the rich people should not have it.

As an example, the corporate income tax probably does not actually bring in a significant amount of money which we could not get by ordinary income tax if the former were repealed. Indeed, it probably reduces total tax collections. Economists in general object to the corporate income tax for several technical reasons. The tax motivates the corporation to put as much as possible of its effort to raise capital into selling bonds rather than common stock because the tax falls on the dividends but not on the interest paid on the bonds. Increasing the percentage of capital represented by bonds makes the corporation more risky because a fall in earnings may force the company into bankruptcy. Thus the economy as a whole is less stable with a corporate income tax.

Unfortunately, the common man likes it because it appears to take money away from the wealthy. When economists point out that a larger amount of money would be derived by taxes if the corporate income tax were repealed because it would increase the total collections from the regular income tax by more than the 'loss' from the corporate income tax, they are usually criticized by the common man. In part this comes from skepticism about the calculations of the economists; but in part is just a desire for the wealthy to have a lower after-tax income even if the cost is a lower total tax collection.

This is a clear-cut case of an envy externality. Morally we may disapprove, and the economist will say that the advocate for the poor is cutting off his nose to spite his face, but we do not have any difficulty in understanding people feeling his way. I see cartoons presenting the common view again and again in the local newspapers because the repeal of the corporate income tax is currently a political issue.

Envy is of course a sin, indeed one of the seven deadly sins. Nevertheless it does exist and it is an example of a negative externality even if I am sometimes guilty. I may feel as an economist that I benefit when a new type of electronic gadget is invented even if the man who invented it benefits much more. Nevertheless, I would rather have some of his money than leave it with him. As an economist, I realize that my living standard is better if large rewards are offered to pioneers, but that is intellectual; emotionally, I feel jealous. Indeed I feel jealous of his intellectual brilliance as well as the monetary reward it gives him.

This externality that upper income people exert on us exists elsewhere too. If you visit Mexico and inquire around, you find that the Mexicans feel the same about almost all Americans. We are wealthier than they are, and for most of us, this is not the result of our own efforts, but of where we were born. I fully understand their feeling, but I'm delighted that they are not permitted to act on it. Few people think of the Mexicans as possible aggressors, but as a matter of fact they feel that we took Texas, California, etc. in an aggressive war, which is correct. If it were not for the vast difference in military power, people living in California would face a real possibility that their houses would be seized by our much poorer neighbors to the south. In fact the reason we are wealthier than the Mexicans is not the fact we seized these areas. The natural wealth of Arizona is no greater than that of the part of Mexico directly south. But what the Mexicans do not realize is that it was American work and social institutions that created the great disparity in living standards. This is easy to understand emotionally. Intellectually it is wrong. If they had the military strength however, they would act on their perception of the world not ours.

The desire on the part of some poor people to share the wealth of some wealthy people exists and is an externality to which government policy could be addressed. In fact, however, we do not observe all poor people receiving large transfers from the wealthy. At the moment I think the citizens in the eastern part of the Congo are the worst off people in the world. They are receiving practically no aid from the wealthy part of world. The people living in the central part of Washington D.C., are much better off and are receiving very large transfers from places that are even wealthier. The reason for this in essence is political. The black population of Washington D.C. can vote in American elections. The black population of the Congo cannot.

So far I've talked in terms of externalities. Let me now turn to another factor, rent seeking.[3] In order to discuss it I must go back to my early work in which I found an error in what then was conventional economics. Economists disliked tariffs and monopolies but normally greatly underestimated their cost to society. I am now about to turn to another form of rent seeking in which the cost to society in direct terms is rather less. When people vote to transfer money to themselves from someone else, there are two costs: first, they may be able to make less productive use of the money than the people from whom it was taken; on the other hand they may be able to make better use of it. If it was used in consumption before it was taken and is used in consumption after being transferred, it is difficult to say whether there is then an increase or decrease in total national well-being. We tend to think that preventing a wealthy man from having a large swimming pool is less of a burden than preventing 100 poor children from patronizing a public swimming pool. On the other hand if the wealthy person was to use the funds for investment purposes we might think that those were more socially valuable than the municipal swimming pool.

The general problem of whether it is wiser to spend money now or invest it has traditionally been left to the individual. I cannot solve the matter and will not make any effort to do so here. If we take money which otherwise would be invested and give it to someone who will spend it, the next generation will be worse off. In terms of simple consumption, the present generation will be better off. It is a trade-off between consumption now and consumption in the future. To repeat, we normally make no effort to impose a decision on people, but as a byproduct, our tax system may change their decisions. In particular, taking money from well-off people and giving it to the poor, insofar as our welfare state does so, will lower our rate of growth and make the next generation worse off. They probably will still be better off than the present generation.

I do not think that these considerations play any major role in decisions to help or not help the poor, but a comprehensive discussion of a matter must at least mention them. Having mentioned them I will leave the matter aside for the rest of this book. Readers may make up their own minds on the matter or, for that matter, also leave it aside. So far as I know, there is no way of determining the optimal investment rate and thereby determining the optimal rate of growth. If readers can solve this problem I hope they will tell me or, better, publish a solution.

In part, then one of the motives for income redistribution is a simple case of externality in which I am made unhappy by the poor circumstances of other people who may be close relatives, distant relatives, friends or even strangers about whom I happen to be informed. The victims of the flood in Venezuela would be in the latter category, but so would citizens of the United States who are badly off. There is, however, another motive, which I think, can be listed as simple selfishness. I suffer an externality by the existence of other people who are better off than I. It is not common to mention the latter motive for income redistribution or at least it is not common to refer to it as an externality. Further, if part or all of their income is transferred to me, I will be better off. In my opinion the bulk of government income transfers are motivated by this rather simple fact. I do not doubt we feel sorry for the poor and are willing to help them, but I note that the help that we distribute to people who can vote is vastly greater than the amount we distribute to people like the citizens of the Congo who cannot vote in our elections.

Our government makes transfers to people who are not well off or who might become less well off without the transfers. We also make sizeable transfers to people who are well off, like the farmers. All of the developed countries have sizable programs to raise prices of agricultural commodities produced by farmers. I have little or nothing to say in favor of our program, but it is less extortionate in injuring non-farmers than the programs in the European Union, Japan or Korea. I suppose that the worst single example of this kind of transfer to a well-off minority is the sugar support for the southern tip of Florida, which primarily accrues to a single family. Still, in net, we do not plunder the food consumer as badly as do various other countries.

In all cases these large transfers to well-off farmers represent simply the political power of the farmers. It is true that when these programs were first started in the United States, the farming community was not as well off as it is now. Nevertheless they were far from the poorest people in our economy. Further the poorest people in the agricultural sector, the black sharecroppers in the south, were actually injured by the program. The owners of the land where they sharecropped did well, but they were already reasonably well off even if they felt sorry for themselves. Of course at the time our agricultural program got well underway, the sharecroppers were black and couldn't vote. That their interests were largely ignored is not surprising so long as they lived in the solid south. A great many of them moved north and the city machines not only let them vote but encourage them to do so if they voted 'right'. It was this more than the later Supreme Court decisions which so greatly improved the situation of the blacks. The original farm program, although it did help white farmers in the Midwest and other areas where there were few blacks, helped the southern landowners more.

Notes

1. I do.
2. Occasionally extreme egalitarians suggest that we could tax the rich in order to bring the incomes of the poorer parts of the world up to equality with us. Of course the amount of money would be greatly insufficient and they rarely suggest that they themselves should be impoverished to bring their income into equality with that of the poor parts of the world.
3. A more complete discussion will be found in Chapter 9.

8.   A survey of the existing system

In this chapter, I concentrate attention primarily on a description of what, in fact, governments, and in particular the American government, do in responding to externalities. The work will to a considerable extent draw on the model I developed in my earlier book, *The Economics of Income Redistribution* (1997). In a way it will be merely descriptive rather than theoretical, but it is necessary to devote some space to why we do the things that we do.

A modern welfare state is partly simply a continuation of the old-fashioned government activity to help people who are in a particularly bad state. In our own history, this was originally done primarily by churches, but it switched to local governments quite early. The modern system however involves a drastic series of changes, which, as I pointed out earlier, in essence were pioneered by Bismarck who was attempting to defeat the socialists in Imperial Germany. Ironically the whole program was taken over and expanded by people who call themselves socialist. Further, at the moment it is almost all that is left of socialism. Government ownership of economic facilities and the planned economy are not currently fashionable. All governments including socialist governments, are attempting to unload the economic enterprises which they own or operate. Predicting (as Sam Goldwyn said 'particularly the future') [1] is difficult and I do not want the reader to feel he or she can depend heavily on my predictions. Nevertheless I think that assuming that the present arrangements will be continued and perhaps expanded, is the safest procedure.

I will devote most of my attention to what goes on in the United States. This is because I know more about it than the other countries, but I will from time to time deal with places like the UK and Germany if they differ from our system radically. Basically, the welfare state, which is to such a large extent the legacy of Bismarck, falls in four general categories. There is first, a pension system for the old, then there is aid for people who are ill. In this latter case the American system is less generous than in many other countries, although this may be in course of modification. There is also some system for helping people who are simply poor, more often than not because they are unemployed. Finally there is a large collection of more or less miscellaneous activities such as, to quote one from the daily newspaper, making efforts to prevent killer whales from sharply reducing the population of seals and sea otters.[2]

Let us take these programs up one at a time starting with the old age pension problem. In order to explain that, I would like to produce a little mythical account of a mythical country. Suppose then, that there was a country in which everyone went to school and was supported by their parents until the age of 20. They then worked at a standard wage until the age of 65 when they retired. They died at 80 having lived 15 years on their savings and interest. We assume that their savings and interest payments were such that they could continue spending during their retirement much the same income as they had spent when they were working.

At this point Bismarck, comes along with a proposition. He suggests that they stop saving money and that the state tax them enough to pay old age pensions for the people now or to be in retirement. Since they will not receive interest on their savings this would superficially appear to be less desirable than the previous system. The Bismarckian system however,[3] will in practice, increase the pensions more or less as the per capita national income grows. Some accounts of the scheme say that the tax payments are investments in the national income and increase as the national income increases. This is assumed to grow, not as fast as the interest rate, but not very much slower. Thus they will do as well, almost, as if they had saved money. The tax will be about the same as the previous savings, but note that everyone who had savings accumulated when the system was adopted, can now spend them without reducing the amount of money they will receive in their old age. If we assume the rate of growth is the same as the interest rate they would be very much better off. Further if they regard government as completely dependable and insurance companies as not so, they might feel they have been greatly benefited.

The question of the reliability of private investment possibilities, for example insurance companies, is, of course, an open one. Companies do go bankrupt, or at least make mistakes in investments, which lower payments. This is a genuine risk. In the twentieth century however the prospect of a government going bust has seemed to be much stronger. Long periods of inflation or short periods of extreme inflation may sharply deteriorate or even abolish government pension schemes. The real value of the dollar is now only about 10 percent of that when the Social Security Act was first enacted. Congress has however raised the pensions so that there is no great loss.

The present situation of older people in the former Soviet Union is a good example of the unwisdom of putting your faith in princes. They are not the only ones of course, shrinkage of government programs through inflation, radical political changes, or foreign conquest is quite common. One of the reasons that Chile's President Pinochet was able to replace an old age pension scheme with a private investment system without causing revolution was that the inflation and other types of mismanagement had led the present value of the existing government pension schemes to being so low that their funding with government bonds injured practically nobody. One cannot depend on private banks or insurance companies, but then also, one cannot depend on the government. Not putting all your eggs in one basket has always been good advice.

To simplify exposition let us assume that, in my mythical country, GNP growth is exactly the same as the interest rate. This would mean that the amount of saving and the annual tax needed for the private version and the pension paid after 65 would be the same under the two different types of provision for old age.[4]

Thus the introduction of the scheme by Bismarck benefits everyone who was old enough to be paying the tax or saving money, but the benefit is larger for older people than the young because they have more savings, which can now be spent.

The scheme however is a trap. Any proposal to increase the tax and the pension or other benefits, provides a gain for everyone who was old enough to be paying the tax since at least part of the tax will have been paid at the previous rate and the new pension will begin at 65.[5]

On the other hand, any proposal to reduce the pension injures everyone much over the age at which the tax begins to be collected since that part of tax already paid is not returned to them by the cuts. Thus the system is a trap causing continuous pressure for increases and continuous resistance to cuts. But note that one standard suggestion for improvement, moving the retirement age upwards from 65, since people now live much longer and are strong enough to work much longer than before, benefits no new retired and injures everyone who has begun paying the tax. Both the total pension amount and the total tax can be cut but that part of the tax which has already been paid will not be refunded. There is no amount of money accumulated from previous undistributed taxes to make such payments (Tullock 1997).

Life expectancy beyond the age of 65 was very low when the old age pension scheme was inaugurated and is now much higher. Further most older people continued working if they had jobs (it was in the Great Depression) rather than retiring at 65. Indeed there was very little retirement in those days except for people who were very well off. Older people tended to take light jobs and a great many of them lived with their children. Both of my grandmothers died in our house. They did various things around the house in the latter years so it is not possible to say whether they were genuinely retired. On the other hand, they appeared to enjoy doing light housework and grandchild care.

The scheme, which we have adopted, does very little in the way of equalizing incomes. When it was first enacted in the United States the pension paid was to some extent affected by the taxable income of the person who retired. This feature has been largely eliminated but it is still true that upper-income people tend to live longer than lower income people and hence draw more money from the social security system. The tax is a percentage of wages with an upper limit, although Bismarck, a brilliant politician, succeeded in convincing most wage earners that their employers paid half of the cost without deducting that amount from the worker's salary. There is a maximum tax no matter what your salary so the system is not strongly progressive.

This amounts to what I call 'horizontal redistribution'. For the average worker the amount that he gets back, actuarially computed, is about what he put in plus interest. But this average is a little odd. Those who die early have a pension, which terminates with their death and hence they receive much less than they had paid in. Those who live long, get more than they paid in. Of course, the fact that some people pay in almost nothing because they are unemployed or at least poor does reduce their pensions. Still the system probably works a significant redistribution from the upper-income people to the poor. Whether this is as great as the redistribution from those who die early to those who live long is not clear. Milton Friedman used to say that it was a compulsory purchase of a poor insurance policy.[6] Actually it is not all that poor, although I do not think we could sell the program to voluntary purchasers. Even people who feel strongly that the system is desirable and use their votes to maintain it probably would not purchase it voluntarily.

In most countries this program is the most expensive income redistribution in their whole system. It primarily helps the old and injures the young and has relatively little other effect on income distribution. I think its great popularity is because the bulk of the population gain when it is instituted since they will begin getting their pension without actually having paid for most of it and it would injure very large numbers of people when it is canceled because once again the losers are mainly people now alive, in essence almost everyone who is older than say 25. Except for the difference between interest payments and the rate of growth, nobody over his lifetime is injured prospectively by the continuance of the scheme.

The same thing can be said about changes in the program. An increase in tax and pensions benefits everyone who was old enough so that the amount that they will pay in tax is not as great as the properly calculated value of the pension. This is almost everyone. On the other hand any reduction in the program injures everyone except the very young who have not yet made much in the way of payments into the fund. Of course the benefit or loss is less for people who have only just begun making payments and large for those who are about to retire or actually retired.

I would like to re-emphasize my opinion that the principal reason for the general popularity of the program is Bismarck's decision to claim that half of the cost was paid by the employers. Apparently the average worker is not aware of the fact that he or she is worth less to the employer if the employer must pay their half and hence their wages are reduced so that they in fact pay both halves. As a matter of fact the employer submits a single check into the fund, but that is not apparent to the worker.

Looked at from the standpoint of the whole economy, there is very little loss. Presumably, people save less money with the system than they would with the previous one, and hence the rate of growth of the economy and of course, the living standard, is somewhat lower after the system has been in place for a reasonable length of time. This however is an indirect and not easily computed cost and I believe most people who vote on the subject are in ignorance of this actual cost. In the early days of the Clinton Administration a medical program with 80 percent of it paid by the employers was proposed. It failed but if my recollection is correct, the fraud of saying the employers would pay most of it was not noticed by the bulk of the people who in reality would pay the cost. Bismarck was in fact a political genius.

The second major reform of Bismarck was in the field of medicine. In order to explain it I must go into a little medical history. Before about 1880 the place of germs as a cause of disease was little known and doctors and hospitals engaged in fairly large-scale transmission of disease from the sick to the healthy. It is likely that the first stage of Bismarck's medical reforms providing medicine and hospitalization for people who were ill, raised the death rate. Fairly quickly after this time however the germ theory of disease was put forward by one of Bismarck's fellow countrymen and doctors and hospitals began an almost fanatical drive for cleanliness in order not to transmit germs. This did not greatly help in curing diseases, but sharply reduced the rate of contagion. It also meant that surgery was much safer and much progress was made in that area. Still in general, people who were ill and who did not require surgery could not be significantly treated in those days. They might be more comfortable in the hospital but their recovery would not be speeded much.

In the 1930s, there was a great medical revolution. I remember seeing a neighbor sitting on her front porch and looking poorly. I asked my mother about it and she said it was pneumonia. At first I did not believe her because in those days pneumonia meant four to six weeks in hospital and a 40 percent chance of death. When I questioned her further she said, 'There is a new drug'. It was sulfanilamide. We called them miracle drugs, and indeed granted the medicine became available just a few years earlier, they were miracles. Of course sulfanilamide was only the start. Today doctors have at their command large numbers of drugs that are poisonous to germs but not to human beings. Germ diseases, which had been the big killers throughout history, now became relatively minor. There are still a few germs we cannot deal with and there are still major dangers, particularly from viruses, but the world has changed very rapidly in this general respect.

In Germany, government-provided medicine became a major factor in health. The system was copied by many other countries but not immediately the United States. We did not get general health insurance or government programs until after World War II. Even today government programs do not cover most people who are under 65 and have enough money that they do not fall into the charitable programs.

Before turning to our present system, I would like to talk a little bit about the situation before World War II, when I was younger. In the first place governments, mainly local governments, did provide hospitals and free access to them for the poor. Further doctors did not charge fees for the poor. I remember the best hospital in my town was run by the city and charged fees for those who could pay, and the better doctors usually sent their patients there. The poor, however, if they did not have a kind of disease that would continue forever, were also sent there. If they were permanently disabled there was another facility also maintained by the city which would provide maintenance for them. Since most such people were elderly, it was called the old people's home. I was never inside it, but externally it was quite an impressive building. Somewhat similar facilities are still available. In general, they are paid for as part of the general social security system.

In the United States a rather intriguing development occurred during World War II. To repeat an earlier discussion, the American government like many others, paid for the war in part through inflation. In order to conceal the fact that the government was inflating our currency they installed a price control and this extended to wages. With a sharp shortage of labor most employers would want to increase wages in order to obtain more workers. Strictly speaking this was illegal, but a way around was suggested. During the 1930s, hospital and medical insurance had developed in the private market. In a deal with the unions it was agreed that employers could purchase medical insurance for their employees in spite of the wage controls. Further the value of the insurance was not included as part of the employees' income for tax purposes. A private citizen who wished to purchase medical insurance on his own would have to pay income taxes on his total income and could not subtract the cost of the medical insurance from his taxable income. I am sure that none of the people who worked this out in the war realized what the long-run consequences would be.

In any event the tax arrangement was continued after the war.

This meant that people who were hired by companies that were large enough for the insurance companies to be willing to sell medical coverage for the entire group without physical exams, got medical insurance with the cost taken from their pretax income. The people who were self-employed or employed in small companies had more trouble in getting this kind of medical insurance. They could of course get medical insurance on an individual basis, but since they had to use post-tax income for this it was quite expensive. Further, various state legislatures enacted bills, which made it impossible for insurance companies to take the medical condition of their potential clients into account efficiently in calculating their premiums. As a result privately purchased individual insurance was quite expensive and many people who felt they were in good health did not buy it.

Most European countries have government-provided health plans for almost everyone. The United States moved a few steps in this direction by providing health insurance for people over 65 and for people who were certified as being suitably poor. All this left fairly large numbers of people without any health insurance. It was not the result of any planning but an outcome of a series of programs taken individually and without any effort to make them coherent.

There was however a fourth health plan. Most hospitals have emergency rooms and Congress ordained that they must accept anyone who presents themselves and provide full treatment for them until they are cured or transferred to another hospital with suitable facilities. The hospital is permitted to bill these people, but it is hard to collect unless they have insurance. In consequence, the cost of this hospitalization is paid by the customers in the rest of the hospital through higher bills. Since many of them have health insurance this means that the premiums paid on such health insurance, either by the individual or by his employer, are higher and hence private purchase of such insurance is even less of a bargain that it would be otherwise.

This whole system is a mess, but we cannot blame Bismarck for it. A movement to complete coverage like most of the rest of the advanced world seems likely in the future. Thus this is one area where the American system does not closely resemble the other welfare states.

Long ago Buchanan pointed out there was a political difficulty in the system. When you are ill you want the best possible treatment, which will be expensive. When you are well you want economy in government. At any given point in time there are more people who are well than under treatment. There are more votes for economy than for luxurious treatments. In consequence there is an almost continuous political problem. Long waiting lines are complained about, as is inadequate treatment. The Fraser Institute in Vancouver publishes annual statistics on waiting lines for serious treatment in Canada. One of the results of their publishing them is that the waiting lines have shrunk even if they are longer than people needing heart surgery would like. Almost all countries go through alternating periods of being worried about inadequate treatment and about unnecessary expense. It should be noted that private insurance companies face some of the same problems and there is no reason to believe they handle it better. It is intrinsic in the nature of insured medical treatment.

Medical treatment is both ideal for insurance and impossible for insurance. The frequency of diseases for the society as a whole is actuarially computable and thus is suitable for insurance. Unfortunately, there is what is called by insurance companies 'moral risk'. It is endemic in medical areas. We discussed it above in the desire of individuals who are sick to get as much treatment as possible. To repeat this is an intrinsic problem of medical insurance whether provided by the government or privately. It gets more publicity however and causes more protests when it is a government program than when it is private.

To relieve the reader from the generally discouraging nature of this discussion let me recount an amusing incident. Canada has a law prohibiting the payment of private fees to doctors or for other medical services. Since most Canadians live fairly close to the American border, this is not a great problem for most of them. It is even possible to buy medical insurance in Canada which will pay for medical bills in the United States, so this rule is merely an inconvenience for many citizens. CAT scans however are an expensive diagnostic tool. When I first became aware of this problem there were more in Tucson where I lived then, than in the whole of Canada. These machines however were not in use 24 hours a day in Canada because the health insurance program only paid wages for a limited part of the day. It occurred to some veterinarians that they could rent these machines during the period when they would otherwise be idle, to diagnose dogs. The *Wall Street Journal* ran a story in which they said dogs could get CAT scans in Canada but human beings could not necessarily do so. This caused a scandal and the Canadian government took immediate action. They passed a law against using CAT scans on dogs. I do not know whether they can still be used on cats.

Canada is not far out of the mainstream in this respect. Most government programs for providing medical attention have at least some rules attempting to prevent people from using private physicians. In general, upper-income people tend to seek out private treatment rather than take the government program and apparently governments feel this will damage the reputation of their medical attention. Germany is an exception here in that there are formal legal provisions for upper-income people to avoid the government program. Mostly however, governments frown on this even if they are unable to prevent it completely. Whether this more expensive medical treatment available for the wealthy is actually better medically or perhaps merely socially and in terms of comfort, I do not know.

We now turn to a medical problem which undeniably involves externalities and which has throughout history inspired governmental action. This is contagious disease. At the time of writing this about the subject, SARS has been getting a great deal of publicity. In fact it is minor compared to things like the Spanish influenza epidemic at the end of World War I, or a number of continuing diseases like measles. So far it has not gotten very much out of China where it originated and the total death rate has been in three figures. Nevertheless it deserves attention and the current criticism of the Chinese government does not come solely from people who dislike that government on other grounds. We can all hope that the scientists will discover a cure.

Meanwhile, let us discuss the general problem of contagious diseases and suitable government activity to prevent their spread. When I was a boy, the so-called childhood diseases were widespread and dealt with by legal quarantine measures imposed on the family where there was a sick child. The health official would appear with a sign, which was nailed to your door and nobody but family could then enter or leave. Apparently the legal provisions were never repealed. So far as I know, no enthusiast for less government, not even the anarchists, objected. It is clearly a case where the externalities are great and the only body, which can impose quarantine, is a government. In addition to quarantine, immunization is frequently possible by inoculation of one sort or another. When I used to travel in the Far East, every time I crossed a national boundary health officials gave me a shot. Not even the fact that I had diplomatic immunity permitted me to skip this mildly painful process. Further I have no doubt that they did reduce death rates in some areas from some diseases.

In general, inoculation or other preventative measures, involving putting something into your bloodstream, do have their dangers. Normally these dangers are very small but not zero. A worldwide campaign to wipe out smallpox by inoculation of everyone within many miles of a given case was highly successful. Unfortunately some nations retained the virus for possible use in future wars. As another unfortunate characteristic, the inoculation process carried a small but non-zero possibility of serious illness. In consequence, the rules which existed when I was a child, requiring every baby to be inoculated were removed because the danger from them was thought to be greater than the danger from the almost-totally-eliminated virus. Today the danger is returning as part of the possibility of terrorism. It is now very difficult for governments to compel people, particularly adults, to get the inoculation and hence there may be a recurrence of this particular plague. No doubt the objection to inoculation will rapidly disappear if the danger of the plague becomes obvious to the ordinary citizen.

There is however another case in which a disease was almost wiped out and then recurred because the popular objection to the preventative measures. By widespread DDT spraying, malaria-carrying mosquitoes were largely exterminated and with them, malaria. The health authorities thought that they had won the battle, but then they found there was another battle, and this one they lost. A woman named Rachel Carson wrote a book called *Silent Spring*, which was a general attack on insecticides, particularly DDT. The word, 'malaria', is never mentioned anywhere in the book and indeed the apparent concern is for birds. Malaria has come back, indeed more than a million people, mainly children in Africa, die from it each year. The power of the environmental lobby however is so great that mass spraying with DDT is rarely even mentioned in this connection. It has been suggested recently that Africans should be taught to use sleeping nets sprayed with DDT at night. Simply spraying walls of the African's huts would also help. Still it is unlikely that we shall return to the near-zero malaria death rate in the near future.

There are other areas where externalities suggest government activity in disease control. A new medicine can be developed privately for sale and there are large corporations giving their entire attention to this problem. On the other hand, basic research in disease generally speaking cannot be sold in the private market and clearly has positive externalities, if it is successful. A proposal that private companies do applied research about medicines and the government engages in basic research in this area is easy to make, but it is rather difficult to draw the line in many specific instances. I think it could be argued that our present system makes an effort to deal with illness by this particular type of division of labor. It is hard to say for certain, but I suspect that some line of reasoning like the one above is basic to the current organization of the medical research community. In any event, I can think of nothing to recommend in the way of improvement.

We now turn to the final section of this chapter. Unemployment has been a problem for many modern countries. It is unfortunately a complex problem, because any effort to provide income to the unemployed will lead to their motives for working being weakened. Suppose for example that we pay $10000 a year to every unemployed person. They are unlikely to accept a job at $5000 a year, but they are also only weakly motivated to accept a job at $12000 a year. After all, many jobs are tedious and tiring, if you only make a gain of $2000 a year, it is hardly worth the trouble. Thus the unemployment payment may well increase the amount of unemployment. Balancing whatever we think is the minimum income that an American citizen or British subject should get against the likelihood that it will provide for some people a motive for remaining unemployed, is difficult.

In the present-day world, and where badly enforced restrictions on immigration exist, a sizable part of the potential labor force in any given country may be illegal immigrants who are in fact delighted to be permitted to work at the minimum rate or less, which is well above what they could make in their native country. Although they are willing to work at less than the legal minimum wage, their employer will break the law if he hires them. It is a difficult problem which is usually blamed on whoever the illegal immigrants are – Mexicans in the United States and Turks in Germany.

The fact that the minimum wage is high enough so that not all employable persons can get jobs is undesirable, but the existence of unemployment payment which is too high is worse. Apparently, in both Germany and France, there are a fair number of people who have decided to make a career of being unemployed and living on the dole. This would not be the first time. In the 1920s, England was in general very prosperous, but it had a large-scale unemployment problem. Economic research seems to indicate that the basic problem was simply that the 'dole' had been placed too high.

In general, we should hope that the unemployment payment will not get that high; but cutting it is always hard politically.

Not only do the unemployed object and cast votes against the politicians who cut, but the labor unions also object. It seems likely that both France and Germany are suffering from a severe problem of this sort, particularly since their unions are powerful. In addition, in Germany at any event, once you hire someone it is very difficult to discharge them. Under the circumstances it is hard for somebody who is unemployed to become employed because potential employers feel that if he is unsatisfactory they will be stuck with him. This also weakens his motives for hard and skillful work since the employer cannot penalize poor work.

In the United States, and for that matter in most western countries other than Germany, it is possible to fire people even if it is difficult and tedious. We should keep in mind that making it hard to fire people makes it less likely they will be hired in the first place, but some kind of balance between these two factors can be worked out. The other problem, that the unemployment payment may be high enough to deter people from getting work, is more difficult. In this case the United States has recently introduced a new and revolutionary technique. If the person on relief gets a job his relief payment is not completely cut off immediately. It is reduced, but the former relief client will receive a net income higher than he received while on relief. Suppose, for example, that he was receiving $10 000 a year on relief and he gets a job paying $12 000 a year. His relief payment will be reduced by $6000 so he would net $16 000 and the $6000 may well pay him for the tedium of working. Note that he might be willing to take a job to pay less than the relief payment. If he took a job paying $8000 a year his relief payment would be reduced by $4000 so he would end up $4000 a year better off. This is a new and experimental procedure and I hope it works.

The more traditional method was simply to make it illegal for him to turn down a job. Vagrancy was a crime. This seems to have worked reasonably well in the United States. Taking care of the unemployed and poor was a local responsibility provided either by the county or city governments in the

United States before the New Deal in the 1930s. Liebergott (1976) collected data from the census and found that from 1830, when his figures start, to 1960 when he stopped, unemployed persons in the United States received an income slightly less than 30 percent of the 'wages of common labor'. Note that the New Deal made no difference except that the cost of the whole thing was taken over by the federal government.

In this chapter, we have gone over the main topics in the so-called welfare state. These activities do not involve externalities except insofar as feeling sorry at someone else's poverty or suffering generates an externality. This is an extension of the conventional meaning of 'externality', but not I think, one that will offend the orthodox. In most modern states, expenditures on this area are greater than those used to generate what used to be called 'public goods'. There is however a very special feature of these expenditures. We feel sorry for poor people in our own country and for poor people abroad. In fact, however, we provide very much less in the way of aid for people abroad than for people in our own country. I think there can be no doubt that the basic difference is that the people and our own country are able to vote and to engage in other kinds of political activities which means they receive more money than foreigners. But this will be the main theme of the next chapter.

Notes

1. Long ago when I first heard this phrase I was told it was by Goldwyn. It is in good accord with his normal linguistic difficulties. Recently, however, I have heard it attributed to other people including at least two Nobel Prize winners.
2. Note my use of the term 'killer whales' instead of 'orcas'. For a considerable time progressive people insisted on using 'orca' rather than 'killer whales'. In the *Washington Post* article which alerted me to the problem, there was a return to 'killer whales', presumably because of the bad behavior of these dangerous sea mammals in attacking other protected species with much more efficiency than wolves attack deer.
3. Here I do Bismarck an injustice, since the one he originally set up was much better than the one I will describe, but it developed rather quickly into the one I will describe.
4. Readers can easily make the mental corrections to bring the model into

correspondence with the actual situation. If they don't want to bother, I can assure you that the changes would be small.

5. If we assume that the GNP growth is slower than the prevailing interest rates and there are no bankruptcies, then the break-even point would be a few years after the beginning of the tax eligibility. To repeat, readers can easily correct for whatever differences they want to assume between these two rates.

6. Milton Friedman, www.uncommonknowledge.org/winter/421.html.

9. Rent seeking

In the last chapter we noticed that transfers of income to do not always go to the poor. In fact most of them do not. The externality inflicted by people who are in trouble may lead to our granting them funds or other assistance. But the amount we give cannot be explained solely by that particular externality. There is another explanation, which is simply that people use their votes or other political means to obtain transfers to themselves. This is not simple and requires looking into a relatively new field in economics, 'rent seeking'. Since I was the one who first discovered rent seeking, although not the title, which was introduced by Ann Krueger (1974), I am in a particularly good position to explain this. I will start with a simple straightforward explanation of what I might call the traditional view of rent seeking and then make some modifications, which are necessary for our current problem.

Traditional economics textbooks explained monopolies with a figure like my Figure 9.1. There is a competitive price and the monopoly raises the price to the monopoly price shown on the figure. Traditionally the shaded triangle, A, C, B which shows the consumer surplus lost by people who would have purchased a product under the previous price and do not with the higher price. The rectangle between the competitive price and the monopoly price D, E, C, A shows the transfer of revenue from the purchasers to the monopolist. The traditional reasoning found in most elementary textbooks says that this is not a social cost because the monopolist is a member of the society, and his gain exactly matches the purchasers' loss. My students normally objected to this line of reasoning because they did not like monopolists. I also do not like monopolists and am happy to say that I can now prove that that line of reasoning was wrong and monopoly inflicts costs on society.

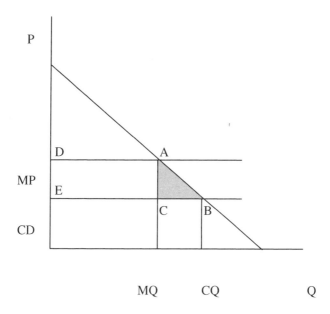

Figure 9.1   Conventional monopoly figure

The problem with this, of course, is that very large amounts of money seem to go to people who have made no investment in getting them. This is possible, but we do not normally expect that in economic activity. Profits are normally the result of some kind of investment, either a physical investment or intelligence and hard work. Where was that in this figure? Superficially it appeared that one could become very wealthy without any investment at all. That seems unlikely. The first solution to it was very hard to get published, in fact my article was turned down by the two leading journals and one mid-level journal before I found a lower-level journal, which would take it (1967). After several years, Anne Krueger reinvented the idea in a much more limited scope (1974). The idea then rapidly spread and now will be found very frequently in the economic literature.

My original article did not say where this would be found in the actual economic statistics. We could explain how large it was, but could not put our finger on the actual statistics. For a number of years I was worried about this problem, but apparently no one else was. It seemed remarkable that, let us say a tariff on steel, could be very profitable to the steel companies and their employees without their making any sacrifices to get that privilege. But where were the costs?

This was a difficult question and for many years I had no answer. I lived for much of this time in Washington in the center of the largest rent-seeking industry in the world. The elaborate lobbying structure in Washington was large but nowhere near large enough to account for the total cost of the special privileges generated. To use my favorite example, I used to drive by the dairy industry lobby building. It was a sizable building but surely could not account for the very large amounts of money taken from consumers of milk, many of them babies, and transferred to a not-very-large collection of very prosperous farmers. The Florida sugar industry was even more remarkable, but I never saw their offices.

There is also the fact that in general, American Congressmen cannot accept open bribes. They do not live in poverty, but if they had conspicuous consumption of let us say $1 million a year, their opponent in the next election would point this out and they would be retired to private life or to jail. This is not to say they do not make physical benefits from the lobbying industry but the amounts of expensive dinners, expensive blondes, and vacations in the Caribbean are nowhere near the benefits that they in fact distribute. It certainly looked as if the special interests like the farmers or the steel industry or, and this is of more interest at the moment, the elderly pensioners, were getting a great deal for a rather small investment. This can happen in the economy but we do not expect it.

This problem puzzled me for a long time but apparently very few other people worried about it. One who did was the Secretary of the Treasury, Sommers, who called me up and asked why I had not solved it. Fortunately this was long after I had begun worrying about it, but only shortly after I had finally found a solution. This solution is the trade of political favors for other political favors. As a result of living in Tucson I know of one particular hideously wasteful project, the central Arizona project, a canal taking water almost 400 miles, which undeniably got votes for our elected representatives in Washington but could not possibly have been passed on its merits. There are other such projects: the Tulsa ship canal, the canal paralleling the Mississippi, almost any part of the farm program. The congressmen who vote for them take credit for the ones that benefit their own constituency and hope that the voters in that constituency are badly informed about others. This may be the reason that constituents usually like their own congressmen but dislike Congress.

I have said very little about campaign financing but this is also involved. The total amount spent in campaign financing is, in general, very small compared to the benefits, which the people who pay it achieve (Ansolabehere et al. 2003). It should of course be kept in mind that these payments are not actually for the purpose of buying votes. The votes are bought by the bills passed by Congress, or the Legislature, which benefit voters. But the campaign money is used to inform the voters about what their congressman has done. Since the voters pay little attention, concentrating the message on a narrow scope and repeating it again and again is necessary even though it annoys intellectuals. On the whole it is the actual things done for the voters by the votes of their and other congressmen, which attract voters to elect those congressmen. The campaign finance is necessary to let the voters know what the congressman has done for them and if possible prevent them from learning the price he paid to get special legislation for them through.

I formerly followed the usual custom here and referred to logrolling only in those cases where the project itself is of dubious value. In fact the same method is used to get valuable projects through. The voter is as likely to reward the construction of a much-needed bridge as a tariff on steel. Indeed, I should emphasize that on the whole we benefit greatly from government behavior, even though it is easy to criticize specific projects. Most intellectuals, including myself, can easily make a list of government projects, which make a negative contribution to our well-being. There is no doubt, however, that looking at the government as a whole we make a very sizeable benefit. The Tulsa ship canal is a minor payment for very great gains which we make elsewhere. Of course we would like to eliminate these wasteful projects without handicapping the desirable ones.

But these are specific and rather narrow benefits. There are a lot of farmers but far fewer than the number of people drawing old age pensions. Further although there are well-organized lobbying groups working for the older people, the 'gray tigers' for example, they devote more time to motivating their members than to directly dining with congressmen. There are, of course, so many people who are over 65 that if they can simply get all of them to vote they have an immensely powerful political organization. Unfortunately, or fortunately, the people who are over 65, if they think about the matter, will realize that if they refrain from voting or vote for a party which is not in favor of the pension system (if there are such parties) it would not make any measurable difference.

The explanation is logrolling. The word 'logrolling' is an American colloquialism. Since I hope this book will be read by non-Americans a few words of explanation are in order. Basically logrolling involves vote trading. A Senator from Arizona will agree to vote for a bill making Tulsa a deep-water port if a Senator who represents Tulsa will vote for the central Arizona project. There is another project which involves, more or less, building a canal which parallels the Mississippi about 300 miles to its east. All three of these projects are highly wasteful for the country as a whole, but benefit a specific area. They involve taxing the whole United States for a rather small amount per capita in order to spend large amounts per capita in three specific areas. The net effect is that the United States as a whole was worse off than it would have been had these projects not been funded.

If the projects were widely known then people living in other areas would vote against them, and they would represent a majority in the Legislature and the projects would fail. Note that I listed three immensely wasteful projects but, to repeat, occasionally some of the logrolling projects are individually desirable. The two senators from Arizona not only got the central Arizona project through, they also got funds to widen an interstate running through Tucson which was very congested. Logrolling is a basic congressional technique and while it does bring many totally wasteful projects into existence, it is also used to fund useful improvements. If we had some way of eliminating the wasteful projects while keeping the good ones, we would be much better off.

One of the problems here is that most voters only know of the projects which directly benefit them in their own area. Under our Constitution, taxes must be general so it is hard to put specific ones down to the area benefited by a given project. If we could, there would be far fewer of these wasteful projects. If the voters were perfectly informed they could deal with the problem by simply selecting the best general project rather than individual ones. Unfortunately, the cost of becoming generally informed is great and it is unlikely that voters will ever incur them.

It is true that the voters tend to feel that they are getting a bad deal, even if they can think of no specific improvements. Public opinion polls normally show that voters like their particular congressman and dislike Congress. The apparent reason is that they credit their congressman for getting special benefits for their local area. The total tax cost is blamed on Congress as a whole. Thus logrolling benefits the individual congressman but not the system as a whole. If the reader has a remedy I think he or she should share it with the world in general.

The word 'logrolling' is American but the practice is universal. All voting bodies use it. I have no information about the internal functioning of the College of Cardinals, but I feel sure that they also trade votes. Certainly faculty voting bodies engage in it, but in most cases they deal with matters which are of stunning unimportance, and hence do not put much time and effort into vote trading. I should say that, although faculty senates deal with issues which are normally of little importance, and hence little time is put into vote trading, there are frequently strong emotions involved. I should confess that I almost never attend faculty meetings, so perhaps my evidence here should be discounted.

In addition to the innumerable minor trades, there are some cases of general coalitions which always vote together without making specific agreements in each case. The labor unions, the blacks, and the Mexicans are some examples among many. There is usually a good deal of trading within the coalition in order to decide what the whole coalition will vote for but they then cast what comes close to a block vote. Probably, the most important of these coalitions are the recipients of various government payments like the old and the people who are dependent on government medical care. And in this case what is being done is usually reported by the newspapers so that those people who were injured know about it. In this sense it is less objectionable than the small-scale trades we have dealt with above because the people injured by the small-scale trades never actually know of them. They only know that their taxes are high.

In the United States the practice is relatively open and everybody knows about it. In other countries, the activity is more covered up, but that does not mean that there is less of it. As an example, I knew a British politician, who was not only in the House of Commons, but became Minister of Education. Since I thought logrolling was universal and all voting bodies used it, I asked him about it one night over dinner. He said, 'Nothing like that occurs in the English government'. The following day he gave a speech on what goes on the House of Commons. He said, 'You go to a committee in which you are totally uninterested and vote with a friend. You then take him to your committee and hold up his hand.' I naturally challenged this and he replied, 'So that is what you mean'. I do not think he'd misunderstood me, but the whole thing is so undercover in the British government that he did not even think of it in the context of our dinner conversation, but when trying to explain what went on a day-to-day basis he produced it out of his hat.

Voting bodies sometimes attempt to make logrolling illegal. Many American student governments have rules against it.

Normally these rules say one should vote on each subject independently and not make trades. Needless to say if an important matter comes up in the actual voting, trades are made. Indeed it is likely that the rules against trades were obtained by logrolling. Even these organizations composed of idealistic students who have nothing very much in the way of material gains to make from their vote are dominated by logrolling.

Long ago when Buchanan and I were working on *The Calculus of Consent* (1965), I did some research for it by looking at a sizeable set of elementary political science textbooks. None of them directly mentioned logrolling, but they did cover it in a very indirect way. They would have a section on how bills get through Congress. The sponsor of the bill, they would say, wrote the bill carefully including clauses he thought would attract votes and eliminating provisions, which he thought might turn off individual members of Congress. In addition, they all said that at the end of the process the sponsor 'picked up a few votes that other members owed him'. Clearly this was logrolling although the name was not used. I suspect that the reasons had to do with somewhat cloudy ethical principles. Today all this goes under the name 'rent seeking'. Whether you like the phenomenon or not you must concede that it is important in democratic decision-making. In order not to show prejudice against democracy, however, I must say that it is also common in royal courts. Various courtiers make trades and form alliances just like congressmen (Tullock 1961). Simply dipping into the voluminous memoirs written by courtiers in any royal court will give you evidence of that point. There are also a lot of accounts of what goes on in the higher reaches of the official circles around modern dictators. Hitler is particularly well documented. At the moment there is little of similar literature dealing with Stalin, but with time there surely will be lots of it. I have been recently reading about Cicero in the last days of the Roman Republic and I feel that he would have been completely at home in the House of Representatives except that there he and his colleagues would not have had to worry about being killed. Altogether rent seeking and trading of favors is universal. It is not at all obvious that it is a bad thing either.

This chapter has been devoted to something that we all know occurs but which is rarely described carefully and accurately. I sincerely hope that this tendency to keep the whole matter under wraps is dying out, with a result that we will know more about it in the future when students turn their attention to it at a higher level of concentration and knowledge than has been the practice to date.

10. War

Warfare is seldom discussed under the heading of externalities although it certainly does impose serious costs on people other than the citizens of the acting nation. I suppose one could argue that since the costs and benefits accrue to the nations participating in the warfare they are not really external. Still innocent bystanders can be hurt and even a purist will except that as an externality. For present purposes, however, we are going to count injury to either of the parties, if it is caused by the other or by the conflict itself, as an externality. This includes the taxes imposed to pay for the war, and conscription.[1]

It seems quite possible that I would not have included a chapter on war had it not been that our war with Afghanistan and the second war with Iraq coincided with my work on this book. Indeed at the present moment both are only winding down. Anyone who has read a history of Great Britain's first three Afghan wars will realize that they never really ended. Britain won all of them in the strict military sense, but in each one found itself unable to impose its terms on the apparently defeated enemy. Afghans are tribal and the defeat of some tribes or even their complete annihilation, as the Russians found out much later, does not necessarily terminate the hostilities. We are now learning that from our own experience.

Our Afghan operation was, militarily, a tour de force. Originally operating off carriers 1500 miles from their target areas and with only the few tribes of the northern alliance for assistance, we were able to destroy a reasonably well-armed and fanatically courageous enemy. Now, however, we face the dispersed tribes in what may be an almost unending guerrilla war. I presume that our generals are reading the history of the British operations in these areas and feeling, at least to some extent, pessimistic.

Our objective however was to get rid of Bin Laden and al-Qa'eda, and we have at least winkled them out of their lairs. Further it seems likely that when they notice the destruction we have worked on the Afghan and Iraqi governments, no other Arab government will be willing to give them open shelter. Thus, we can say that we have won a principal objective. Unfortunately, terrorism is hard to deal with. The sect of the assassins did, after all, operate in this area and imposed a reign of terror from what is now called Tajikistan to Egypt for over a century. They were finally disposed of by the Mongols who used regular military forces. In our case it is likely that the CIA will be more important, although the military forces will, of course, be necessary (see Lewis 1987).

That the terrorists could impose externalities on us no one who watched TV on September 11th will doubt. We then imposed great costs on them. In both cases many innocent bystanders suffered severe injuries which we can consider externalities. This is unfortunate, but normal in warfare. This particular kind of warfare which is of necessity fought in areas where many outsiders are present, is particularly rich in generating externalities. So rich in fact, that the citizens of Iraq are now complaining about the damage to their living standards inflicted by our troops. Indeed, it looks as if the US military government is significantly incompetent.

But it is always easy for a professor, sitting quietly in his office in the United States, to judge the activities of people holding real responsibilities and working under extremely unfavorable conditions. There is however, no reason why I should not exercise my freedom of speech by criticizing. You, the reader, can exercise your freedom by either ignoring me or writing me nasty letters.

But let us turn to more normal warfare. It is usually a costly business for the citizens of both the warring nations. But the costs of the war inflicted by a government on its own citizens are a different order of externality than the damage inflicted by the enemy nation. Heavy taxes to pay for war effort are normal in wartime, both for countries on the defensive and for those which are attacking. Further, many wars are, from the perspective of the attacker, morally correct, with the result that the citizens may not think of themselves as engaging in aggression even if they are attacking.

Some people think that the country which is attacked must defend itself, and hence has no choice about imposing heavy costs on its citizens to pay for the war effort. There is, as a matter-of-fact, no reason why they must fight. They can simply surrender. We have a sort of natural experiment here. After Germany and Russia had disposed of Poland, Russia attacked the former Baltic provinces of the former Imperial Russian government. The difference in military forces available to Russia and the four former Baltic provinces was immense. Three of them, Latvia, Estonia and Lithuania simply surrendered without fighting. One of them, Finland, chose to fight.

Granted the odds, that decision to fight may have seemed unwise. Finland lost a great many soldiers and ended up losing one of its most important cities and a large part of its economically important real estate. It did however remain independent and democratic. When Hitler attacked Russia, the Russians, obscurely motivated, attacked Finland. Finland responded and their army showed its ability to work as well in the offensive mode as in the defensive. They not only recovered all of the land taken by the Russians in the first conflict, but they pushed a good distance beyond those borders.

When it became clear that Germany was losing, Finland tried to make peace with Russia and the Russians permitted them to do so without taking very much real estate that had not been occupied by the Russians previously. There were some German troops in Finland at the time and the treaty of peace required the Finns to dispose of them. This led to a short but significant outburst of fighting with the Germans. After the war, Finland was saddled with truly immense reparation payments to Russia. Although the United States was mildly sympathetic, we did nothing in the way of really helping them.

The other three countries that peacefully surrendered had no war casualties. But this was Stalin's Russia, and the secret police immediately began mass deportations. Further, large numbers of Russians were moved in as settlers and the economy was of course taken over by the occupation forces. When Germany declared war on Russia, they occupied the three Baltic states and attempted to set up governments that would be friendly to Germany. This led to a great many people within those governments being disposed of when Stalin returned.

In this natural experiment, it is not at all obvious who did best. Certainly when Russia collapsed the conquered areas regained their independence, but were much worse off than Finland. Whether this loss made up for the losses in Finland during and immediately after the war is not obvious. Speaking for myself, I think Finland was right in its choice, but this may be an expression of my bias against the Soviet system.

There was another sort of natural experiment in Scandinavia. Norway and Denmark surrendered. Sweden declared neutrality while making it clear that it would fight defensively. A strong military machine, together with the fact that a number of high-ranking Nazis liked Sweden, led to their being undamaged. Of course they paid heavy taxes to support their military machine. Norway and Denmark were totally unprepared for war and their surrender was almost certainly required by this situation.

In this second natural experiment, it is once again not clear who it was who came out best, but I prefer the Swedish solution. I should perhaps point out that if Germany had not succeeded in taking Norway, the British would have done so. They actually began an occupation operation when they suddenly discovered the Germans had anticipated them. Instead of occupying Norway, they attempted to get the Germans out using more or less the same troops and other military forces that they had prepared for their invasion. I would imagine that the Norwegians would have surrendered as a supinely to them as to the Germans. The Dutch and the Belgians of course fought and lost.

The point of this little history is simply to point that it is not necessary to get into war to defend yourself. That is a decision and the costs of surrender can be regarded as an externality

inflicted by your own government instead of another externality which a defensive war with taxes and casualties would have
inflicted.

It should also be pointed out that offensive wars can be very
profitable so they have both the negative externalities inflicted
by the tax and military operations and positive externalities. The
United States is a standing example of the positive externalities
which aggressive war may provide. We are essentially a conquest
society. Almost all of the land which we hold on the American
continent was seized by force and violence from previous occu-
pants. This includes the thin strip along the Atlantic occupied
by settlers mainly from England. It is interesting that difficulties
with the Indians are one of the complaints against the king of
England in the Declaration of Independence. The declaration of
course was signed well after the fighting had begun near Boston.
It accused the king of stirring up the Indians which, probably at
that time, he was doing. It was the new settlers on the western
fringe of the white population who were having difficulties with
the Indians and it would be possible for a pacifist to argue that
if they had not entered the area they would not have had trouble
with the Indians. Granted the existence of warlike Indian tribes,
however, that is by no means obvious.

In any event we continued pushing west and displacing the
Indians until we reached the Pacific. I find in talking to intellectuals about this, that they frequently say we bought part of
this area from the French. It is not obvious that the French
actually owned Louisiana in clear title. After the end of the
war, and the fall of Napoleon, the Spanish argued that they still
really owned it or that at least the transfer was only a strip
along the Mississippi. In any event, the area was almost
unknown to European peoples. We sent Lewis and Clark out
to explore an area which was not only not settled by Europeans
but not even known in any detail. We then started a long series
of minor wars to displace the Indians.

We also took Florida. It was purchased, but only after
Jackson had invaded. The really big war of aggression however,
was the seizure of Texas, California, and the other western states

in the Mexican war. This more or less completed our holdings on the North American continent and we stopped adding land by aggressive wars at that time. Canada we had attempted to take in the Revolutionary War, and again in 1812, but failed both times. We bought Alaska and acquired the Gadsden purchase quite peacefully. In both cases, the only question is whether or not we paid more than the land was worth.

It is notable that although up to about 1890 we mainly engaged in aggressive wars, it is a little hard to say whether our attack on Tripoli was defensive or offensive and the Civil War was of course internal.[2] Since then our wars seem to have been motivated either by moral principles or, more simply, by excitement. The war with Spain might be considered an exception to this. At the end of the war we held Cuba, the Philippines, Puerto Rico, Guam and some minor islands in the Pacific. It is hard to argue, however, that these were the objectives of the war. The combination of the Spanish ruthlessness in putting down a rebellion in Cuba, which happened to coincide with a circulation war among newspapers in New York, and which led them to give a great deal of attention to Spanish atrocities, led to public opinion being vigorously anti-Spanish. Thus the sinking of the *USS Maine* in Havana harbor set off a war.[3]

As for Cuba and the Philippines, in both cases democratic governments were established and eventually the United States withdrew. Puerto Rico has been a minor drag on the United States, and various efforts have been made to make it either independent or a state. So far there has been little enthusiasm on the island for either solution. The Virgin Islands, purchased during World War I, are unimportant and almost totally dependent on the American tourist business. Guam, seized in the war with Spain, was never actually made into a naval base, and its possible potential as a tourist destination has not been developed.

Hawaii is an intriguing special case. Americans, who had migrated onto the island, overthrew the royal government with the aid of a visiting American naval vessel. Their intent was to become a part of the United States, but Congress refused to admit them. They therefore set up a republic with the intent of joining the United States when possible. Eventually Congress let them in.

If we take only the period up till about 1890, there is no doubt that the United States was a successful aggressive power. Further the externalities generated by and for American citizens were significantly positive in total. Even today, we can think back and say we are better off because of the Mexican war and the innumerable Indian wars than we would have been had we followed a pacifist policy. The positive externalities were great and the negative externalities, in so far as they existed, fell mainly on foreigners or indigenous people. The actual cost of our Indian-fighting army was very low, immensely less than the value of the real estate taken. Morally this is not particularly meritorious, but if we look at material outcomes, we did very well.

In the twentieth century whether we did well or not depends on your approach. I am what is called a 'realist' in my views of foreign policy and hence feel we could have done much better. I must admit, however, that my position is very much that of a minority. I even generally approve of the activities of the Marines and the army in the Caribbean, which is as far from the moralistic position as you can get.[4]

In order to avoid misunderstanding, I would like to say that I do not approve of starting and then withdrawing support from the Bay of Pigs operation or the assassination of Trujillo. But these, in addition to killing Diem, are best described as ill-conceived moralistic operations rather than 'realist'.

Before turning to our more important twentieth century foreign policy we may consider a few other cases of aggressive wars with possibly positive externalities. It is not generally realized, but the British, French, and Belgian empires were essentially developed in the nineteenth century, not earlier. It is ironic that at the same time that these three great empires were being built, the older Spanish empire and the equally old Portuguese empire were in states of dissolution. Pieces of them were retained into the twentieth century but the whole of Spanish South America had gained its independence by then. The Dutch empire in the Indies and its holding at the tip of

South Africa were older and indeed held by whites until the disintegration of the more recent empires after World War II. British control of India moved from a few trading posts to one province and then the whole of the sub-continent beginning with the Seven Years War, but mainly in the nineteeth century. Their scattering of other colonies in the Far East were also more recently acquired.

All of these were example of successful aggressive wars. Whether the externality which they imposed on the citizens of their own country who paid taxes to support them was large enough to counterbalance the gains from the empires is an open question. Generally, although the actual fighting certainly caused damage and death, it is not at all obvious that the conquered people were worse off. They had been mainly governed by petty tyrants who were almost continuously at war. The colonial powers did not have to give good government to be an improvement. Leopold's Congo company has a deservedly bad reputation, but reading Stanley's account of his trip down the Congo from the central highlands to the sea gives the general impression that the company may have been an improvement.

The Dutch empire was built by a self-supporting private company, but without the taxpayer-financed navy, would have been impossible. The Honorable Company of Merchant Adventurers also maintained it own army, but could not have held its position, not to mention expansion, without the help of the British taxpayers. Most of the economists in the nineteeth century thought that the empires were losing investments. Thus although many citizens and officials gained externalities in the Empire itself, there were negative externalities imposed on most of the citizens of the imperial powers. It should be noted that because of tropical disease, Africa was colonized very late.[5]

With the possible exception of the Belgian Congo, which was run as, in essence a possession of the King of the Belgians before 1905, few even claimed to be profitable in total. It is of course conceivable that the citizens of the home countries gained in entertainment and feeling of pride in the achievements in their empire to make up for the material costs. Today, many American cities spend a great deal of money to produce a winning athletic team, which, in strict material terms, makes them poorer. Perhaps a knowledge that your local regiment had done well on the Northwest Frontier led to the same kind of euphoria. In other words psychic gains may have counterbalanced material costs.

Looked at from of standpoint of the whole country, the physical externalities were, I think, negative. Further, as I said above, that was a general opinion of the economists of the time. The possibility of psychic externalities, which more than counterbalanced that, cannot be ruled out even though present-day intellectuals receive psychic externalities from the same events in historic memory and regard the externalities as negative. The same intellectuals regarded the disintegration of the empires as presenting them with positive externalities, essentially of a moral nature.

Since 1900 we have engaged in no wars aimed at annexing real estate. It is hard to avoid the feeling that emotion and moralism are now the causes of our recent major wars. The Marine Corps engaged in some minor operations, which seem to have had material motives, but they were unimportant and probably unprofitable. [6]

The two great wars, however, come close to being crusades. World War I was essentially, simply stumbled into by the European powers. Only France, which wanted Alsace-Lorraine back, and Serbia, which wanted a sizable part of the Austro-Hungarian empire, favored the war. It was set off when an employee of the Serbian intelligence service assassinated the heir to the Austro-Hungarian empire. It is still unknown whether this was his own idea, or whether he was acting on orders. The events arising out of this assassination were truly tragic. It was the first war in which the tremendous casualties possible with reasonably modern equipment, were inflicted.

The United States motive for entry had nothing to do with material gain.[7] The English dredged up the telegraph cables connecting Germany with the Western Hemisphere and made use of their near monopoly of transmission facilities to disseminate strong anti-German propaganda. It seems likely however that the principal reason for America entering the war was the explosion of antagonism set off by the German submarines. Granted what American submarines did in the Pacific in World War II, is almost impossible to believe that the German submarines caused our entry into World War I, but that is what President Wilson said, and it seems to be the verdict of history.

The outcome of the war, on the whole, was disastrous. Austria-Hungary was broken up, a true tragedy, and Serbia was expanded, thus clearing the ground for the collapse and vicious internal fighting that we have seen recently. What was left of the Turkish Empire after its military disasters in the nineteeth century was dismantled. Since then we have had two minor wars with one of its former provinces. It is hard to argue that we gained from this. Still on the whole things were not so bad in the 1920s.

With the 1930s came the Great Depression, essentially an American downturn, which spread and which stubbornly refused to go away until we began preparing for the war. In Europe, there was Stalin's famine in the Ukraine, and a great purge of all sorts of people that he suspected of not liking him. Hitler then became dictator of Germany with an announced policy of reopening the war. Japan meanwhile had begun a not very effective, but bloody, effort to conquer China. All this was depressing but did not directly concern the United States. The prospects were bad, however, and perhaps some preventive measures could have been taken. What we actually did was pass the Neutrality Act in order not to get drawn into the next war.

Once fighting had begun in Europe, we made our sympathies clear, but did nothing much until the fall of 1941. We did begin building up our army, navy and air power. Japan had no domestic sources of oil and we worked out a scheme under which the British and Dutch cut off their access to external oil sources by use of naval vessels. We also began escorting ships to England to protect them against German submarines. There actually was one minor skirmish between an American destroyer and a German submarine before we were officially at war. Then came Pearl Harbor, Hitler's declaration of war, and we were in.[8]

If the United States had any material interest in the war, it was to make sure that there was not one hostile power dominating Europe. This was also a very traditional British policy. Since we ended with one power dominating Eastern Europe, we obviously failed. Further we lost all our friends in there. The latter was partly made up by the fact that the Russian occupation in Eastern Europe, and in those parts of China and Korea that they entered, was so unpleasant that in the long run we actually got some friends back although they have little power.

In 1942, I read a book by Schumpeter (1942), which was mainly on economics but he dealt with the war as well. He said it was a three-sided war, and although Germany would surely lose, it was not obvious whether the United States or Russia would win. This cold-blooded approach to the war was not widely held. I know that none of my acquaintances agreed with my view, which was the same as Schumpeter's. Indeed when I was in the army I thought it best to keep my mouth shut on the matter. Whether it was possible for our government to defeat Hitler without turning Russia loose in Eastern Europe was not clear. What was clear is that nothing was ever considered in that direction by the US. Churchill in the privacy of his study worried about it, but nothing was done.

Altogether the external costs of World War I and World War II were high and the gains low. Nevertheless in popular memory, they are great triumphs and of course it is true that, if you ignore the role of the USSR, both did have some aspects of a crusade. But we should not forget that in the long run, the crusades in Palestine themselves failed. Currently, the collapse of the USSR probably means that we are now in good condition, but that is not because of our skill and intelligence in World War II. In foreign policy it is best to think and not to emote.

World War I and World War II were major wars, with large forces committed. Since then, there have been two minor wars without very many troops involved, in Korea and in Vietnam.

In both cases we came out badly, although it can be argued that the Korean outcome was a tie. We unambiguously lost in Vietnam. In both of these cases we had allies who contributed some, but not much, to our fighting power. In both cases the outcome for the people who fell into the hands of the Communists was depressing.

I have not mentioned our two wars with Iraq, or the war with Afghanistan, because they were such minor affairs. All three of these cases, we won easily, although the Pacification was not successful. It is not all obvious that in the long run they will be to our advantage. The second Iraqi war led to a massive mobilization of public opinion against the United States, even among American intellectuals. I suspect that the motive was dislike of the present American government. But that is purely a subjective opinion. Of course, the continuing guerilla war is discouraging.

The reader will notice that I have been largely but not entirely devoted to foreign policy of the United States. I think, however, that I could produce a history of Britain over this period that would lead to much the same consequences. Indeed the end of the British Empire, like the end of the French, Dutch, Belgian, and Portuguese empires shows the same general picture of internal political influence on foreign policy. The view, held by many economists, that the home countries actually lost from the colonies, seems to have had no influence. It was an outburst of moral thinking and in practice does not seem to have much injured the former colonial powers. If we look at it from the standpoint of the former colonies, in many cases, the abandonment of Empire was a catastrophe, but by no means in all. India is doing reasonably well as is Malaysia. Singapore is flourishing. Indonesia is not flourishing but not catastrophically injured. Africa is a disaster. Altogether, here again we see foreign policy dominated by a poorly-thought-out morality, but it is not at all obvious that there was another policy which would have done better.

This chapter has dealt with an area, which is not normally referred to as falling within the scope of externality.

Nevertheless it is obviously true that when a country deals with things outside its own border there is an externality. When dealing with these external factors it is necessary to collect taxes, draft soldiers, and impose severe security restrictions on the citizenry, this is another case of clear externality. If there are gains from it, this is a positive externality. There seems no way of avoiding such externalities, but we can at least hope that the governments will behave more intelligently in this area in the future than they have in the past.

Notes

1. My feelings on this matter may be stronger than those of the reader. I was involuntarily in the infantry during World War II.
2. Some unreconstructed Southerners still refer to it as 'the war of northern aggression'.
3. It is still not clear what caused the sinking. In those days magazine explosions were not unusual among naval vessels, but surely an external source is reasonably likely.
4. See Boot (2002), *The Savage Wars of Peace*. It is a history of various minor military actions undertaken by American forces without a declaration of war. They have been widely forgotten in the United States but South Americans normally remember and resent those which took place in the western hemisphere.
5. So endemic were some diseases to parts of West Africa that a saying arose: 'Bewatch and beware of the Bight of Benin where few come out though many go in'.
6. See note 4.
7. For a highly, on the whole, unfairly, critical account of Wilson's foreign policy see Thomas Fleming *The Illusion of Victory* (2003). It should be said that Wilson's mother was English and his principal foreign policy adviser Col. House had both an English mother and father. It is not obvious that this affected the course of things very much, but it may have. In any event, the United States remained a principal financial source for England during most of the war. The father of Dean Acheson was Episcopal bishop of Connecticut. He and his wife both remained British subjects and Acheson toasted the King's birthday each year in his childhood. Again, whether this made any difference is unclear.
8. Critics of Roosevelt sometimes allege that he deliberately arranged Pearl Harbor. This is ridiculous, but it is true that his errors in disposing the navy provided an opportunity for the Japanese. I am slowly producing a book entitled *Open Secrets of American Foreign Policy*. This will deal with cases in which the conventional wisdom is wrong and starts with a detailed study of Pearl Harbor. It will probably be years before the book is ready but parts of it are on the Web.

11.   Monarchies and dictatorships

So far, we have dealt with various aspects of democratic governments. Most of the human race however has lived under undemocratic governments. Once again, most of these undemocratic governments have been monarchies or dictatorships. Note that 'monarchies' as used in this chapter involves kings or queens who actually do rule, not merely ceremonial figures like the present King of Sweden. Thus Gustavus Adolphus would be counted as a monarch for our purposes, but his present-day successor or the British Queen would not.

In this chapter, I will distinguish between monarchs and dictators by the method of replacement when one dies or is by some other method removed from his position of power. As a norm, monarchy is hereditary while the dictatorship is held by someone who has seized it by force or political maneuvering. We tend to think of the replacement of a king by his eldest son as the norm. In Europe, where there is a sort of social hangover from Greece and Rome, kings had only one legal wife at a time and did not maintain a harem. Thus there was an obvious candidate in the eldest son.

Of course the succession was frequently disputed. The Wars of the Roses in England were set off by such a succession dispute and ended with almost all of the potential heirs by blood, dead. Henry VII who took the throne by winning the battle of Bosworth Field, had only a feeble blood relationship with his predecessors. Nevertheless, he was a most successful, if rather unpleasant, king.

Remember, however, that while succession by the eldest son was normal in Europe it was by no means a world norm. For its successful functioning, insofar as it did function, it required that there be only one legitimate wife at a time. This was a norm in Europe, but certainly not so in other parts of the world. Further the hereditary custom of some particular other race or group might be different. The reader no doubt recalls that Marco Polo returned to Venice by sea rather than crossing Central Asia on horseback. The reason for this is that between the time that the Polos went from Venice to Khambulac (Mongol Beijing) and their return, a civil war had broken out in Central Asia.

Under Mongol custom the heir to a person's property, including his government, was the youngest son not the eldest. Kublai Khan was the eldest son and had seized the throne, at least somewhat irregularly. His younger brother revolted and, since he was the legitimate heir, was able to attract a good deal of military support. As a result, Central Asia was for a number of years a war zone with large well-trained cavalry armies, commanded by excellent generals, contesting its possession. In consequence, Marco could not return by land and had to go by sea. The long-run effect of this war, although the younger brother was captured and executed, was the practical division of the Mongol Empire, with two Western Khanates more or less independent of the central government in the East.

This could not, of course, have happened in exactly the same way in Europe, although smooth and easy succession was not always achieved in Europe either. Normally, however, the eldest son did succeed his father. If there was no eldest son, there were sets of rules as to who would be the legitimate heir. It did not always work out. When Alexander the Great died, his legitimate heir was his half-brother who was unfortunately, feeble-minded. There was a brief effort to install this feeble-minded half-brother in his place and then another feeble effort to select Alexander's unborn son. The crown was actually placed over the Queen's womb, but, of course, this did not really work out. The end result was a war between various generals in Alexander's army usually called the 'wars of the successors'. They were immensely destructive but did not eliminate Greek control of the Middle East and northern India.

Once we turn to rulers who maintain a harem, the situation

becomes complicated. Wars between the sons on the death of their father were common. Selim the Grim, decided to end this problem by a suitably grim expedient. He enacted a household law for his dynasty under which whichever one of his sons achieved the throne was required to kill all the others. The potential heirs spent their youths in a special palace surrounded by eunuchs and women who were thought to be infertile. At the death of the ruler there was a small civil war in that palace and the winner killed all his brothers and half-brothers. This prevented sizable civil wars in the domain of the Caliph, but did not produce a line of distinguished rulers. Other dynasties have used other methods. The Ming dynasty provided a healthy pension for the younger sons of the Emperor, but insisted that they move to palaces in pleasant parts of the Empire remote from the capital.

Whatever can be said for or against hereditary succession, it produces kings and not dictators. The dictator is a man, or occasionally a woman, who fought his way up the slippery pole. He is not necessarily a nice person, in fact, normally is *not* so. On the other hand he is usually a person of great ambition, intelligence, and unscrupulousness. He may or may not be highly competent, Napoleon certainly was. In any event he must watch his courtiers carefully to see that one of them does not replace him. The Grand Captain, Hernandez de Cordoba, won many battles for the king of Spain in Italy. When he returned to Spain the king immediately ordered him to be restricted to his estates. Since they were extensive, this was no great punishment, but it did make sure that he would not replace the king. The family of Pizarro was wiped out by a jealous king and the family of Cortez were made members of the nobility, but carefully kept from achieving real power. This was hardly a great reward for adding so much territory to the domains of the king. I can draw as many good examples from other royal families. Uneasy lies the head that bears the crown. The sword of Damocles is always suspended above it.

The dictator is surrounded by high officials who would like to replace him. Since they are not only candidates for the throne, but also rivals, the dictator can usually, but not always, keep them under control. Designating a successor is obviously dangerous since the other high officials will want to be on good terms with that successor and, hence, may not be completely loyal to the dictator. Normally dictators do not appoint a successor until they are almost dead. One way of minimizing the danger of having a successor is to select someone who can feel fairly secure that he will not be replaced by anyone else, and a blood heir is a good example. If the heir is not selected by the ruler but by some general standard, such as the son of a king, this is safer. A non-hereditary dictator, however, has difficulty here. Still appointing your eldest son may well be the safest thing to do.

If we look at the matter from the standpoint of high-ranking courtiers, although they would individually like to replace the current dictator on his death or, preferably, earlier, most of them however realize that they themselves will probably not make it up the slippery pole and hence attempt to make favorable connections with others who they think have a better chance. This leads to a situation rather like that in the American nominating conventions back in the days when we did have contested nominations for the President in the conventions of both parties. The individual politician wanted to attach himself to the winner, but was aware of the fact that guessing the winner is difficult. In consequence, it is best to hold off endorsement of a given candidate until it is clear he would win. On the other hand, early support was more likely to be rewarded by the winning candidate than a last-minute jumping on the bandwagon. This provided politicians with a very difficult situation, and it is not obvious that they did well in solving it. The courtiers surrounding a failing dictator face the same situation except that an error in this judgment may lead to an appointment with the hangman.

Probably, appointing your eldest son as your heir is the safest way out of this problem for the dictator. On the other hand, the number of kings or dictators who have been killed by their designated successor is not insignificant. If I kill my father in order to be king, I can among other things protect myself against punishment for the murder. This is probably more likely with eldest sons than with anyone else because the former have more security in their positions as heir to the throne than would a simple high official of the regime. Still, the problem is difficult.

At the moment, there are few hereditary thrones, but many non-hereditary dictators. Some time ago in my book *Autocracy* (1987), I predicted that many of these dictators would in fact convert their throne to hereditary succession. So far my prediction has had modest success. The current dictators of North Korea, Syria, and the Congo, are sons of the preceding dictator. Of course, in the case of the Congo, the situation is so confused that it is not obvious that being dictator is of much value.

So much for dictators, but we now turn to kings. Today dictators are quite common and hereditary kings quite rare. And indeed if we leave out a number of minor Arab states, in all of which the heritage of the succession has been very short, we find almost none. Over the broad sweep of history, however, this is the commonest single form of government. Note that I do not intend to separately discuss ruling queens. There have been a few and some of them like Elizabeth I of England were quite important, but their methods of government and control seem more or less the same as those of kings. It perhaps should be noted that royal governments tend to be more favorable to women as rulers than democracies. Female queens who actually ruled are far from unknown, while to date female presidents have been nearly non-existent. Still the number of female rulers whether queens, presidents, prime ministers, or dictators is very small.

Let us then consider what I would call the normal case of the hereditary king. The actual founder of the dynasty is apt to be a man of considerable capacity. He has worked himself up the slippery pole as has a dictator. He normally will therefore be exceptionally intelligent, hard-working, and politically adroit. Granted the accidents of gene selection, his son's abilities are apt to be much less deviant from the norm. In intelligence, drive and political ability they probably do not differ very much from the average voter. Thus in both democracy and monarchy we are ruled by mediocrities. In both cases, of course, the actual officials and advisers are well above average intelligence, drive and personality, whether they are advising the monarch and governing by direct contact, or dealing with the mass of voters by way of newspapers, TV and talk radio. Thus in both the cases of democracy and hereditary monarchy, rather ordinary people are brought, at least to some extent, under the influence of far-from-ordinary advisers and officials.

The king, of course, has received specialized training as a child. Much of this training is in the problems of government, but unfortunately much is also in expensive ways of entertaining himself. He will also have formed connections with a number of people who hope to be high officials in his reign. There are occasional hereditary kings who are truly outstanding. Alexander the Great will do as an example. There are also hereditary kings who were distinctly subnormal. Louis XVI of France and Henry VI of England are examples. Mostly however the distribution of ability, ambition, and moral principles among hereditary kings is probably not greatly different from the similar distribution among the voters.

The French monarchists developed a rather good argument for absolutist royal government. We tend to think that, if there is a king, his power should be restricted by the Constitution, but the French monarchists did have a pretty good argument for absolute rule. Putting it in our language, not in theirs, this eliminated externalities and rent seeking. No doubt they were over-enthusiastic, but they did have a point. If the king is the absolute owner of his country then any expenditure comes out of his own pocket and a benefit derived from those expenditures comes to him directly. He pays to build the road, but the completed road is his property. In a way he is like a citizen deciding whether or not to pave the driveway to his garage. He pays for it, and hence has a motive to save money, but he then will make use of it and hence has a motive to put in a good driveway. Both the cost and benefit fall on him.

The situation is rather like that in a large corporation the stock of which is held by one man. The Ford Motor Company would do as an example. When the king or the owner dies, the country or company is taken over by the eldest son. We do not object to this in the case of the corporation. In practice, the son is frequently much less talented than his father. In consequence, he normally either runs the company into bankruptcy, sells it, or transfers control to someone else. Those cases in which the son of the founder of a large company retains control and runs the company efficiently are quite rare. They are, however, not non-existent. We do not worry about the damage to our economy by large companies being transferred from exceptionally efficient founders to less-efficient heirs, but this is partly because the less-efficient heirs will normally be put on the shelf quietly and without much difficulty. Replacing an inept king is not as easy and is more likely to have bad effects. The problem is obviously more serious with monarchies, but the fact that many dynasties have lasted for many generations without disaster indicates that it is not fatal.

In a democracy much the same argument of the French monarchists can apparently be applied to the whole body of voters. But for the individual voter there is no connection between expenditure on an asset and the benefit of which he derives from that asset. Most citizens would like to have various streets improved. I regularly complain about Interstate 66, which I regularly use, being only two lanes each way rather than three or four. If I were asked to pay for it, I would certainly give widening it more careful thought then I do now. I might reach the same conclusion, but certainly the decision would be more carefully thought out.

We regularly use arguments of this sort when we assume that private businesses make more careful calculations than the government. A corporation deciding whether or not to build a new store, factory, or access road is far more likely to make accurate calculations than is a government body eventually dependent on voters whose share of the burden and of the potential gain is for each individual very small. Of course government officials are in a somewhat different position, but they retain their jobs by pleasing the voters. Further they do not have to please all of them. They do not even have to please a majority for any particular project although they will lose their jobs if the sum total of their activities displeases a majority. Further the individual voter has no significant motive to either collect information actively or to think about the matter carefully. That is not true of the king. Although the king may well make mistakes, at least he has the right motives when considering investing in his kingdom. Like the average voter, the king may be extravagant and pay little attention to anything except to the direct benefit he achieves. In that he is again like the average voter. But we will return to the issue of royal extravagance later.

As can be seen, the absolutist king makes his decisions in a situation in which there are no externalities. Everything is his. A new road costs money which comes out of the royal purse, but the benefit of the road also accrues to the king. If it is a successful investment, his tax revenue will go up enough to more than compensate for the cost. If it is not successful and that must happen many times, he will be out of pocket. Putting the matter in our previous vocabulary there are no externalities here. He cannot impose costs on others not because he is generous or wise, but because all of the costs and benefits of the kingdom accrue to him. The fact that he is absolute gives him, in these matters, the right motives even though he may not be intelligent enough to make the correct calculation.

Most likely he has an IQ not too different from that of the average voter. His ability to calculate then is not great but not zero. The fact that all benefits and costs fall on him, however, does tend to lead him to make quite different calculations than the average voter who faces only a minor share of either of these and may consequently not know much about one or the other. In essence, this argument of the French royalists points out correctly that the king has the right motives in making government expenditures. This is clearly an advantage, but it is not obvious that this alone is enough to justify absolutism.

We now turn to specific criticisms of royal governments. The first is that they may be extravagant. No one who has visited Versailles, or better yet the palace complex in Peking, which makes Versailles look like a mud hut, will doubt that kings can spend a great deal on their own accommodation. The kings of France also spent a good deal on their mistresses, but nowhere near as much as the emperors of China spent on their numerous wives. On the other hand, these are big countries, particularly China, and it is not obvious that the cost of these palaces was a greater share of the total national income than the great amount we in the US spend supporting our legislative and executive branches in Washington. This is not really a fair comparison since the Congress performs functions not just like those of the king, but also those of many of his courtiers. Still, it is not obvious that the expenditures on luxuries by wealthy people in the United States, cannot be directly compared with those of kings.

I should here introduce an observation of my own which may or may not be true. Most people, and that includes kings, have rather limited imaginations. Once the king has a palace twice as large as that of the wealthiest of his subjects he is unlikely to think of anything in the way of an additional luxury. Versailles is big, but much of it is government offices or other parts of the government. If we subtract these, it probably is not much larger than some of the chateaux on the Loire. The kings may be extravagant, but they normally lack the imagination to waste very large amounts of money. The Field of the Cloth of Gold is frequently listed as an extravagance on the part of the kings of France and England. It could as easily be listed as an expensive effort to achieve foreign policy goals without war.

This leads to a discussion on war, which was frequently referred to as the hobby of kings. It is certainly true that absolutist government frequently engaged in rather pointless wars. Unfortunately the same can be said of democracies. At the moment of writing we have forces in Iraq, which are being very heavily criticized by intellectuals almost everywhere, but particularly in Western Europe. Further we are considering sending troops to Liberia. In this case intellectuals seem in general to be in favor of the operation.

If we go back in time, the wars of the French Revolution certainly were as wasteful as any royal wars. The extension of the empires in the nineteenth century was largely carried on by countries, which if not fully democratic, were moving rapidly in that direction. The abandonment of the empires in this century has largely been done by democratic countries and I think most people who look at it will argue it was no more intelligent than the building of the empires in the last century.

Still many very warlike states have been monarchies. Timur the Limper was a monarch and killed an extraordinary number of people. The Mongols, and he was descended from them, also were mass murderers. But most monarchs have not engaged in this extravagant behavior. The most destructive wars in history were fought in the last century with democracies important participants. Indeed in World War I all of the major participants were either democracies or would soon be so. This does not mean that monarchies were not warlike only that democracy also is warlike.

I find that in talking with ordinary citizens about monarchy, their criticism is largely something they picked up in school. Myself, I do not favor monarchy, and I prefer democracy although as you will discover in the last chapter, I can think of the number of modifications which would improve it. Nevertheless I feel that normally people object to monarchical governments mainly because they involve a sharp change, not because they have carefully considered the matter. This does not of course mean that change to monarchy would be an improvement. Indeed I think it would be a serious mistake. But I do think we should give more thought to different forms of government than we normally do.

There is a sort of intermediate stage between royal governments and democracies. This is most easily understood if we consider feudal Europe. The king depended upon his lords in that most decentralized of government organization for not only running local government but actually providing him with his army. If he wished to attack a foreign country, defend his own country against such attack or suppress a rebellion he simply called on his nobles to bring their train of warriors to his camp. He had himself a considerable number of men at arms, but not enough to win a major war. Under the circumstances he would be wise to consult with his high-ranking nobles before invading a foreign country or resisting an invasion. Whether he had a formal council or simply called up the nobles in case of emergency would be an optional decision.

As a result of this problem, most feudal monarchies usually had some sort of more or less formal collection of high-ranking nobles upon whom they relied for advice and military support. Most of the readers of this book are more familiar with English history than any other and English kings certainly had this problem. Somewhat similar bodies existed, however, in almost all of the kingdoms in Europe. The kings with widespread domains might have several such bodies in different parts of them. Charles V of Spain and Germany faced some 22 such small bodies and spent much time travelling around Europe to solicit funds from them. Normally the councils started as only high-ranking nobles but with time tended to add on groups of commoners who had money and who had better be consulted before the money was seized.

As we all know, bad King John failed to adequately consult his high-ranking nobles and they formed a coalition against him and at Runnymede he was forced to sign the Magna Carta. It does not seem however to have made much difference in the relations between the King and his high-ranking nobles. I doubt that it caused any improvement at all in the situation of common people. Insofar as they were oppressed, it was local nobles who caused them difficulty, not the King. In reading the document I have always suspected that what the nobles really objected to in the section on trials was that the King was trying noble lords before juries of common people. In any event that became illegal under the Magna Carta.

A considerable time after Runnymede, Simon de Montfort, Earl of Leicester, led a revolt, which failed. In the course of the revolt however, he asked each county in England to send two knights to consult with him. After he was defeated and killed, the king decided that this was a good idea and continued the custom. This is the origin of the House of Commons.

Historians frequently argue that the House of Commons and its gradual development was the origin of modern democracy in England. The development was however very slow and until the reform of 1842, real parliamentary power was held by noblemen who sat in the House of Lords or in some cases wealthy commoners who had purchased seats in the House of Commons.

The house of Pitt held six seats in the House of Commons in fee simple absolute. Two of these were the representatives of Old Sarum, a plowed field which sent two representatives to the House of Commons. Since the prime minister in much of the wars set off by the French Revolution was one of the representatives of Old Sarum, the system cannot be regarded as a disaster. This was one of the major emergencies England faced and with another prime minister it might not have survived. Even if he was irreplaceable, the navy would probably have still won battles and Napoleon would have invaded Russia. Still, it is hard to argue that the system which not only won an important war on the continent but also presided over the beginning of the Industrial Revolution was totally bad.

In his book *The Structure of British Politics at the Accession of George III* (1957), Namier describes the situation in considerable detail. As a result it is one on the more amusing of serious history books. To take one example that impresses me, a group of public-spirited citizens in a North English constituency auctioned off their two seats which were purchased by London merchants. This whole project was widely approved in the constituency because the money derived was used for road repair. Whether this can be regarded as an early form of democracy is obviously questionable.

It was not only nobles and wealthy men who selected members of the house. Cromwell, the Lord Protector, on one occasion ordered Col. Pride to physically remove 50 members of the house whom Cromwell suspected would not obey orders. Most of the kings were not quite so arbitrary, but they certainly intervened in the election process. Altogether, although historians are no doubt right in saying that the House of Commons was the origin of British democracy, the development up to 1842 when there was a major reform was certainly very slow.

But it should be emphasized that consultations between the king and his courtiers were by no means always so evenly balanced. To take one example, the Persian emperor would call a large body of advisers to meet with him and offer advice. When he thought that he had enough advice he would announce his decision saying, for example: 'It is my will that we invade Athens'. The courtiers would then chorus 'it is the Emperor's will' and the matter would be finished. This is quite different from the assent that modern constitutional monarchies give to the acts of their parliaments.

As a general rule the king and council form of government is not stable. In England the council, i.e. the two houses, gradually reduced the king to a mere ceremonial figure. The same thing happened in most of the other countries of Europe, which are called 'constitutional monarchies'. The process usually took considerable time and there might be temporary regressions, but the general procedure was to shift to a democratic government. But this is not always true, the shift can go the other way. Louis XIV simply told the Estates General to dissolve itself and go home. His order was of course obeyed. Later Louis XVI attempted to revive the Estates General and lost his head in the process. In this case, there was no gradual movement but two abrupt changes. The only case I know in which there is a king and a council with both having at least some power is the current kingdom of Morocco. Based on the historic experience, I would imagine that this will either move to a democracy or to a more despotic king.

There is another form of government which looks peculiar, but in at least one case has been very successful. The Pope appoints a board of Cardinals to advise him and to carry on some of the work of administration. When he dies, they elect his successor. Although the system does not work perfectly it has worked pretty well. The fact that all of these high-ranking officials of the church are required to be officially childless may be one of the reasons it has been successful.

The interesting feature of the system, from our present perspective, is that the Communists had seemed to be moving towards adopting it. Stalin appointed the Politburo and then when he died they elected his successor. Later the Politburo actually removed one 'Secretary General', but in general the system has not worked as well as in the Catholic Church. It is possible to argue that the Communist government of China has followed the same rule. Deng Hsiao Ping was more or less elected by a similar body although, as in the Russian case, there was a pro forma meeting of the legislative body, which normally is a complete cipher.

Deng retained considerable power even after he had formally retired. When he died, much the same thing happened again, but not so smoothly. I am perhaps in a small minority in regarding the present government of China as somewhat unstable. Whether it works out well, which is what almost everybody thinks will happen, or whether it fails as I suspect it will, is at the moment in the hands of the gods.

The system has a superficial resemblance to a cabinet government in a democracy. The resemblance is only superficial, however, and whether it will actually become a genuine cabinet government is, I think, very doubtful. A permanent government in which the existing ruler appoints the advisory board, which will select his successor, failed in Russia. It also failed in all of the public governments in Eastern Europe, but in those cases the whole thing was a fraud from the beginning. The Russians actually appointed all of the formal leaders in those countries. With the collapse of Russia, some of these leaders were able to acquire real power. Turkish language group leaders of Central Asia have been able to convert their previous bureaucratic position into a genuine dictatorship, but I doubt that this is permanent.

This survey of the standard form of government of the

human race, a ruler who may seek advice but does not have to follow it, is brief. Further, I cannot claim to be a profound student of the area. My advantage in talking about it is simply that most other people concerned with this form of government have tended to ignore everything except some form of democracy or some form of monarchy.

Just before my first visit to Venice I encountered a friend who had just completed his first visit. He was enthusiastic and said that every church was worth going into, and every second building was worth stopping and looking at. Although I did not actually stop and look at every building in Venice I certainly enjoyed the collection of splendid architecture. It was particularly impressive because not only is it beautiful, it is quite an engineering achievement. All these buildings some quite large, some being tall towers, and all are built on a sandbar. The fact that they could build these structures whose foundations are piles driven deep into the sand shows both artistic taste and engineering abilities. The fact that it was hundreds of years ago makes it more remarkable.

Venice started as part of the Byzantine Empire and only gradually moved from rule by appointed delegates of the Emperor to a government, which is usually referred to as Republican. From about AD 1100 until about 1800 they were ruled by a Constitution, which does not much resemble any other. Granted their great success under this Constitution, it is sensible to consider it carefully. Note that the only other government, which remained in undisputed control for a similar period, was the Royal House of Korea, which governed for almost 600 years. Korea however, was a very special case because of its subordination to China. No other government comes even close to that record. For royal governments, as I have emphasized above, normally the succession was interrupted from time to time and the dynasty replaced by distant relatives. Since it worked for a long time and produced good results, I think it can be commended, but I can think of no way in which we could carry out further experiments on this procedure. Still, the view that our present form of government is ideal seems to be mainly the result of custom and conservatism. I feel that we should seriously consider possible radical changes, and I devote the next chapter to this subject.

Venetian cultural achievements in the form of art, mainly during the Renaissance are remarkable. In spite of its poor geographic location, Venice is one of the true beauty spots of the world. Today of course it attracts mainly tourists but its non-touristic achievements were for many generations far more important. Their cultural advance in many fields was remarkable. They were pioneers in printing for example, and Galileo and Vesalius were professors in their university during the time of the most important of their scientific discoveries.

Economically their merchants were very important in the Near East and their navy put the pirates down in much of the Mediterranean. They were important in the founding of modern banking and for many centuries their currency was the safest in Europe. The modern diplomatic services took the Venetian embassies as their model. We all know that Marco Polo went to China and eventually produced the first information on that great empire that most Europeans had. Altogether, this was a major center of civilization for a long time.

But these were from the Venetian standpoint lesser accomplishments. They built a sizable empire in the valley of Po and an even larger empire in the East and the statement that they 'stood firm guard against the Turk' is only a little exaggerated. In fact they were forced by a series of wars to slowly retreat. Given the difference between the size of the Turkish empire and the domain of Venice, it is surprising that they did as well as they did. Europeans can look back with considerable thankfulness to the long period in which the Turkish threat was largely held in check by the Venetian navy.

I am, of course, a Venetian partisan. The reader may tend to take my praise with a few grains of salt. Still he can hardly deny that their accomplishments were remarkable and the present situation in which a sandbar is one of the world's major beauty spots seems almost impossible.

The point of this brief discussion is that the political system of Venice was also remarkable. For almost 700 years, from the time that Byzantium gave them independence until Napoleon conquered them, they had essentially the same remarkable constitution. It is not true that they did not slowly change, but the average Venetian probably noticed little change over the course of his life. Today we may think their government was bizarre, but it certainly worked.

Whether we call it democracy or oligarchy is a question of definition. Basically a rather small group, probably about 5 percent of the adult male population actually present in Venice elected their government. The requirement for presence in Venice was of some importance since they had many of their citizens out governing their empire or on diplomatic missions. When they returned, of course, they could once again vote.

Not only did this small group of the people elect all of their officials, many took an active role in voting on policy. If you visit Venice, you will see the immense rooms in the ducal palace. That is where the citizens gathered to vote fairly frequently. They not only elected the higher officials, they also debated and voted on policy matters. Granted the fact that many of them were merchants, it is surprising they could spare the time to participate in large public meetings.

Their voting method for electing officials from our standpoint would appear to be peculiar. A large volume of randomness was introduced into the nominations. For a very brief discussion see the account in my book *On Voting* (1998). If the reader is interested in more careful and thorough study he can read *Venice, A Maritime Republic* by Frederic C. Lane (1973).

The point of the large element of randomness was to prevent the family maneuvers which tore apart most of the other Italian republics. The details look peculiar to modern eyes, but they worked. Most of the people voting in such an election would have personal knowledge of the candidates, but, on the other hand, the randomizing process together with the fact that members of the same family could not even be present when a candidate was voted on probably led to competent people being selected. In any event the system was successful for a longer period than any other government of which I have knowledge.

Granted the success of the government and the fact that I admire it, the reader may wonder why I give it so little space. The reason is not prejudice but the fact that I see no possibility at all of such a system being adopted in the near future. Indeed not even in the distant future.

12. What, if anything, should we do?

On the whole the world seems to be in pretty good shape today. Do we need to consider possible improvements? I would not be surprised if the reader answers that question with a firm 'no'. I am however by nature a reformer and so I should like to consider both difficulties with the present world and what we can do about them.

Starting with foreign policy, the United States has just won a minor war, but ended up with trouble with guerillas. We also are currently disliked by the intellectual community practically everywhere. One would think that the Saddam Hussein regime would have no defenders, but while no one except his Minister of Misinformation and a few corrupt ministers defended that regime, there are many people who say that he did not have weapons of mass destruction. Since the elimination of such weapons was one of the reasons given by the American government for eliminating Saddam, even people who do not like him and are pleased that he is now in captivity, are critical of the American policy.

I suspect all of this is simply a reflection of the latent anti-Americanism of many European intellectuals together with the anti-Bushism of many American intellectuals. They now have an excuse for stronger dislike. There is little or nothing we can do about this cast of mind, but it does not seem very dangerous. 'Sticks and stones may break my bones, but names will never hurt me.'

As long as the countries, which are objecting so audibly to our operations in Iraq, have practically no military power, we can avoid doing anything about the matter. It would be nice if they liked us more, and sending significant numbers of troops to help with the anti-guerrilla campaign would be even more desirable. It seems unlikely however that we can accomplish either of these goals.

The guerrillas are, of course, a problem. We can in fact regard the previous terror campaign as simply an earlier guerrilla war activity. Unfortunately, I can suggest nothing much to do about it other than what we are doing now. We should not however expect a high degree of effectiveness in the matter.[1]

I referred elsewhere to Boot's book: *The Savage Wars of Peace* (2002).[2] Much of it is taken up with anti-guerrilla wars fought by the Marines. On the whole, these were in the end successful although there were casualties during the fighting. It seems rather similar to the present situation in Iraq except that there were far fewer Marines and hence fewer cases in which they were shot. With patience I presume we can expect the same outcome, but I am not positive we will have the patience.

The word 'assassin' comes from a Muslim sect which used assassination as its principal tool, both in spreading their particular Muslim heresy and in developing a significant power in the Middle East. Their operations were at much the same time as the crusades, but they did not seriously hamper the Crusaders. DeJoinville in his *Chronicles of the Crusades* (1963) pointed out that murdering a Grandmaster of either of the orders of crusading knights would not have done any good because another would have been immediately elected. The Crusaders' great enemy, Saladin, however paid blackmail to the assassins. Presumably, he valued his life more than Grandmasters did theirs. The sect was finally wiped out by the Mongols.

More recently, the People's Will in Russia carried on a long campaign of assassination in which they got a czar and a great number of junior officials. It was finally wiped out by Stolypin, who introduced military trials and many executions. At about the same time groups of anarchists not directly connected with Russia carried out a number of assassinations and bombings in Western Europe. Among their accomplishments was fighting a small battle in downtown London with a small detachment of the British Army. They finally simply died out. If we are patient, I expect the same thing will happen to al-Qa'eda. I would like to have a better solution to the problem, but I do not. I urge my readers to solve it, but must admit I am not optimistic about their prospects.

If we leave these depressing, but essentially minor problems, aside, the world is currently in pretty good condition. As an intellectual myself, I am particularly interested in the world currents of opinion. Today, democracy and a reasonably free market seem to be widely accepted among intellectuals.

This represents a significant change from the earlier part of my life. When I was at law school in the University of Chicago most of my politically interested classmates were socialists. They tended to be pro-democracy, but the dictatorship in the Soviet Union and other socialist countries did not appear to annoy them. I remember a leading member of my class in the law school explaining patiently to me, an obviously retarded student, that of course the planned economy will grow faster than the free economy, because the central group controlling the economy had complete information about each part of it, whereas in capitalism, managers knew only one part – their own.

This particular defense of socialism is certainly not commonly used today. But the view that with good centralized management we could do better than with the chaos of the market was held by many intellectuals until recently. A friend of mine, Warren Nutter, got a large research grant in the early 1950s to study the rate of growth of the Soviet Union. He found it much slower than the official claims although not exactly contemptible. As a result he was almost drummed out of the economic profession. The CIA, for example, funded two separate statistical studies which came out with much the same numbers as he had, but which criticized him very heartily.

To give two examples of the climate in economics, on one occasion when I met a mutual acquaintance he said 'Is Warren still underestimating the Soviet growth rate.' On a second occasion I found myself sitting next to an economist, who was a stranger, at lunch. I knew that he had done work on the Russian economy and so I began a conversation with him on the subject. He immediately said he could not talk to me because he knew that I was at the University of Virginia and hence knew Warren Nutter, and might be plotting some kind of trap for him.

The University of Virginia moved Warren to an inconvenient office and it was not possible for him to simply shift universities because his reputation elsewhere was one of a person who had done bad, politically motivated, research work on the Russian economy. Now we know that he was right except that he probably estimated the growth rate as a little higher than it actually was.

All this is unimportant except that it was important for Nutter. He was reduced from a prominent economist to a non-person. Fortunately for him he was able to get a senior appointment in the war department. Still a good career was frustrated simply because he was right.

I do not want to argue that this was absolutely typical but it was true that up to about 1980, the view that Communism was working well was dominant both in economics and in the general intellectual community. Further the tendency to ignore the very large death rate under Communism was also strong. Communist governments were not referred to as democracies, but their totalitarian nature tended to be ignored.

I have dealt with all this mainly to remind the reader of the previous state of society. Beginning in the late 1980s all this disappeared. I think the collapse of the Communist state in the USSR and the adoption of capitalism in both Communist China and Communist Vietnam may have been the basic reason for this change. I have never read anyone among the fashionable intellectuals offering any rationalization for the change. Indeed most of them have forgotten the previous dominant intellectual opinion.

Perhaps I devote too much attention to this change in intellectual opinion. I am after all an intellectual myself and hence likely to give greater importance to intellectual matters than would the ordinary citizen. I remember many cases in which I was seriously inconvenienced because of the previous dominant intellectual climate, but never anything that really destroyed or even badly handicapped my career. I am happy about the change and I hope that my reminding scholars of the previous climate of opinion may be useful, but now I will turn to more current issues.

At the moment the United States is recovering from a minor recession. The economy did not seem to respond well to treatment whether inspired by the Chicago monetarists like myself or Keynesians. I find a certain amount of grim amusement in the Democratic attack on deficit financing. After all this would be the Keynesian solution and the Democrats are mainly Keynesians. The monetarist solution has not really been tried but the feeble gestures in that direction by Greenspan do not seem to have cured the recession either.

But we are suffering only a minor recession. A number of other countries are suffering larger ones. Japan, Germany, and France are in considerable difficulties. In the case of Japan, although I am in a way a Far Eastern expert, I do not understand what is wrong. Both France and Germany are barred by their agreement with the European monetary system from undertaking Keynesian deficit finance on a significant scale. Further, both of them, Germany in particular, have arranged their welfare state in such a way that the unemployed have no great motive to seek employment. This does not lead to serious suffering, indeed the unemployed are quite well-off. Thus my general optimism about the present situation does not really apply to our economy, although the problem is minor from the perspective of someone like myself who lived through the Great Depression.

Considering the military situation, we won two wars with Iraq without much difficulty or many casualties. Whether the current guerrilla attacks on our troops will be easily dealt with or not, I do not know, but in any event we can certainly bear them. It is popular at the moment to point out that our military budget is larger than the sum of the nine other countries with large budgets. This figure does not normally include China and is not corrected for the difference in the amount we spend on the well-being of our troops. Further it should be kept in mind that we lost the Vietnam War although our expenditures were surely much greater than those of our opponents and we only tied the Korean War although once again we spent more than our opponents. Thus the apparent conviction of the newspapers that we are all-powerful should be taken with quite a number of grains of salt.

Nevertheless, in addition to the improvement in the climate of opinion on economic matters, we are in pretty good shape in other areas too. General optimism seems warranted, but we should keep in mind that in the past we have been badly disappointed by the change in the economy or international situation.

I would like here to turn to a discussion of our domestic problems, specifically as outlined by Chapter 9 on rent seeking. Long ago James Buchanan and I wrote a book *The Calculus of Consent* (1965) which introduced a series of radical ideas about the functioning of democratic governments. [3] Although these ideas were radical then, many of them are now orthodox. The term 'rent seeking' had not yet entered the normal discussion of government, but a good part of our book would lead to much less rent seeking if the reforms were implemented. In essence they would make rent seeking more expensive to the legislators and hence they would choose to buy less of it. If you have to pass a bill for seven economically unproductive water projects in order to get one in your district, you are less likely to be able to put through the coalition than if you only need three. Of course you yourself might think it too expensive for your own voters.

In general the proposals I shall make below tend to require, indirectly, a somewhat larger majority of the population to get matters through Congress and hence the sponsor would find it more difficult to get pork for his district. I have found that most Americans react with shock at my proposal to abandon simple majority voting. They feel that that is a very essence of democracy. It is sensible then, to pause briefly and discuss whether majority voting actually is so common in our democratic society.

The body, which makes the most decisions in the US society, is a jury, which always votes by unanimity.[4] This is an old custom and I do not suggest we change it so long as we use a jury, but it certainly is not majority voting. There are a number of other cases in which the US deviates from majority voting in making government decisions. At the moment the Senate of the United States is being hampered in its deliberations by a rule, which says that any senator who proposes to filibuster can be overridden only by 60 percent of the Senate.

This rule is interesting because in general the political left dislikes it, but at the moment they are strongly supporting it. Their support began when Bush nominated a judge that they objected to but who would get a majority in the Senate. Invoking cloture rules then became something which leftists could do. At the moment they are a couple of additional cases in which the Democrats are threatening to hold up proceedings by requiring a 60 percent majority to get a vote. In former times it was the political right that used the cloture rule but the left does not seem embarrassed by their current situation.

I read both the *Washington Post* and the *Washington Times* in order to get both sides of the news. Normally the *Post* is on the left and the *Times* on the right. In this case it is the *Post* that is supporting the use of the 60 percent rule for cloture and they do not seem to be at all embarrassed by their reversal of position. They point out that the Constitution specifically provides for each chamber regulating its own procedures. In the past, when cloture was used by Southern Senators to delay civil liberties bills, it was the left that objected. The *Times* does not mention the problem very much, but when they do, they claim that our government is based on majority rule and hence cloture procedure is improper. I cannot recall previous times when they put great emphasis on the sovereignty of the majority.

Another case in which the US Constitution itself provides for more than a majority to back legislation is the presidential veto power. In essence the Constitution provides for a three-house legislature, the president being the third house. If he rejects a bill it requires two-thirds majority in both houses to override him. Whatever one thinks of this provision, and I am in favor of it, it certainly is not majoritarian.

But the Senate itself is probably the least majoritarian part of the US Constitution. Congressmen in the House of Representatives each are elected by more or less the same size constituency and hence represent, or at least were elected, by a majority in their constituency. A majority in the House then, without serious misrepresentation, can be referred to as representing a majority of the voters. This is by no means true of the Senate.

The decision to have two Senators from each state regardless of population was made at the constitutional convention in order to make it likely that the Constitution would be ratified. It was a compromise in which the large states would dominate one house and the small states the other. Looking back from the present I cannot see any reason why we should have criticized this decision. Nevertheless it does mean that a majority in the Senate does not necessarily, represent a majority of the voters.

A voter from Alaska has about 30 times as much power in the functioning of federal government as a voter from California. I doubt that the Senators normally line up large states against small states. Thus it is not likely that a majority in the Senate regularly or even frequently represents less than a majority of the total population. It does happen however. So far as I know, no one has collected data on the point, but majoritarians should be upset by the present arrangement. Since I am not majoritarian, I do not object, but I do think the distribution of political power in the US Senate is undesirable.

Let me now turn to the argument contained in Chapter 16 of *The Calculus of Consent*.[5] There I point out that a diversity in the way the members of two houses are elected can require more popular support even though their representation is equally distributed in each one. To take the example, which I invented for that chapter, which supposes that one of the two houses represents the entire population with equal numbers per senator but the constituencies are alphabetical.

With the population arranged in alphabetical order one senator would be elected by the first 1 percent of that list. Thus each House would, if there were a majority, represents a majority of the population in a true sense. Although this is true, in general, in order to get a majority in both of these houses we would require more than a simple majority of the population as a whole. This would only be untrue if by some wild coincidence, the geographic constituencies and alphabetical constituencies coincided.

Many states have bicameral legislatures with different methods of allocating the members of the legislature in the two different houses. Some time ago the Supreme Court decided that this was unconstitutional in the case of states if one of the houses used radically unequal populations to allocate seats. As they pointed out, a voter in a thinly populated constituency had more power than one in a heavily populated constituency. To take the statement most often quoted: 'Trees do not vote'. Of course we can point out that under the federal Constitution trees do vote in Alaska. Since the unconstitutionality of the unequal representation was derived from the federal Constitution, but applied to the states, this was a rather bizarre ruling.

But then many rulings by the Supreme Court are bizarre. Further when we are talking about majority voting, and the Supreme Court does vote by majority among the justices, no one would claim that they represent a majority of the population. Nevertheless they throw out things that have gone through the more or less a majoritarian part of the government. Here again we have an area where the majority is defied.

As far as I know there are no careful studies. Indeed it would be very difficult to make such a study and I would tend to doubt its accuracy because of the difficulty. Nevertheless I think that I perceive an increase in the total amount of money appropriated by the states since this change occurred. The reader is free to disagree with me on this point, but I would appreciate good data on the matter. Unfortunately I can think of no research design which would be likely to be definitive.

I take it that no one will disagree that the Senate's method of election means that different voters have different amounts of political power, depending on what state they live in. Most students are aware of this but it is rarely given much prominence in discussions of reforms. At the moment there is a very mild upsurge of interest in making the distribution of voter power more equal by a redistribution of the constituencies. It seems to be more a left-wing movement than right, but in any event is weak and it is not obvious whether the right or left would gain by such a redistribution.

My motives are not particularly affected by the right–left problem on this particular issue. I both want the relative power of voters for the Senate fairly close to equal and want to improve the efficiency of the whole system by seeing to it that the two houses are elected by different methods. The last criterion was discussed earlier in connection with rent seeking and that earlier discussion provides the basic reasoning for my proposal.

Many Americans do not know this, but in the world as a whole the first pass the post method of election, which we inherited from England and still use, is a minority system. Most countries use proportional representation for at least one house of their legislature. Sweden, for example, has simply abolished the house that depended on first pass the post so that the proportional representation house has complete unhindered control.

There are two voting methods which are called proportional representation. One of these called the hare method is complicated and is used in Australia but not in very many other places. I will ignore it here, but if the reader is interested it is briefly but accurately described in the *Encyclopedia Americana*.[6] The other method, which is widely used has a number of variants. There is no point in going through all of them here so I shall start with a simple procedure and then go on to a brief discussion of more complicated ways.

Under the system used in Israel and in the Netherlands each party makes up a list of potential candidates for the legislature which is as long as the total number of vacancies. How many vacancies will depend on how the country is divided up. It might be in that the whole country is one constituency, or it might be that the country is broken up into a number of constituencies each of which will get, let's say, 20 seats.

Some central organization of each party makes up the list of candidates with as many names as there are vacancies. The voters then cast a vote for the party and it will receive as many seats as its proportional number of voters in that particular constituency. In a simple system the ones elected will be the ones at the top of the party's list. Needless to say, this leads to very strong party discipline in the legislature.

There are other systems in which the voter may vote for a given candidate on his party list. Or for that matter, he may vote for individual candidates in several parties. In the Swiss system the voter draws a line through one name on the list and writes in one of the others, thus casting two votes for that particular candidate. There are other ways for permitting voters to actually select the candidates from the party list. In this system, or these systems since there are several ways of doing this, the number of candidates a party elects depends on the number of votes for the party, but the individual voter can influence what particular candidates occupy the seats.

This system avoids the geographic mal-distribution which we are accustomed to in the US Senate. Suppose, for example, we use a national constituency with 100 seats to be filled. This would be the same size a Senate as we have now. A majority of these senators would have been elected by a majority of the electors. Under present circumstances a majority may have been elected by much less than a majority of the voters. The individual voter in Alaska, to use my previous example, has much more influence on national policy than a voter from California.

This changed system is fairer than our present method and would not have a bias towards states with small populations. It might be harder to get the agricultural bills through, and that clearly would be an advantage. Further, and this is a feature that attracts me, the coalitions of voters made up to support a given piece of pork in this legislative house would be different than those made up in the House of Representatives which I would leave unchanged. In essence this would effectively require a larger collection of voters backing any particular bundle of proposals which it is thought can be got through by logrolling.

Presently, things like the central Arizona project appeal to senators and representatives from more or less the same geographic area or representing more or less the same pressure groups. By making the representation in one of the houses nongeographic, we make it harder to make up these bundles of projects. Anything which in fact benefits a majority of the population would not be injured by the change. It could pass in both houses.

Once again all this is drawn from the reasoning found in Chapter 16 of *The Calculus of Consent*. I should say that although this chapter is in some ways the most radical of the chapters in a basically very radical book, it has attracted practically no objection. I think this is not because everybody bought the idea, although certainly it was widely approved, but because it did not seem likely such a reform could be adopted. The change that I am proposing, however, not only has this technical advantage it has an apparent moral advantage too and hence would be easier to get through.

Most, but not all, legislatures that use proportional representation for one house and some other method for the other, like Germany, for example, use cabinet-type government with the executive being elected by one house, usually the proportional representation one. There is however, no reason why this is a necessary consequence. We could retain our present arrangements for the executive, an elected president who appoints his own cabinet and has the veto power, while having one of the two houses elected by proportional representation. This would mean that we have two houses of parliament and a President elected by different methods and hence majority support for anyone of them would not correspond exactly with the voters providing majority support for the others. Granted my desire that legislatures differ in their supporting groups, this would be even better.

As a third change here, we could have the President directly elected by popular vote. This would increase the degree to which each voter in the United States had the same power, while making logrolling and pork production harder. I would anticipate then a further improvement in efficiency.

Most people who have not studied the problem think of voting and counting votes as almost simpleminded in terms of mathematics. Unfortunately that is not true. Beginning with the work of Condorcet, and proceeding with Lewis Carroll's investigation, serious students of voting realize the problem is not an easy one.

Black and Newing (1951) show that only by accident could there be an alternative with a majority against each of the others. Arrow (1950) produced a very general proof that there are paradoxes in all voting methods. If we look at the actual history this is obvious. Lincoln and Wilson were both elected by surprisingly small percentages of the popular vote. Both Kennedy and the second Bush got, not only less than half the total vote, but fewer votes than their opponent. As an extreme case the current president of Argentina received only 20 percent of the popular vote in the only election in which he stood.

But these problems of voting paradoxes infect all known methods of voting. We may regret them and hope for some mathematician to solve them. For the time being however, the sensible thing to do is to ignore them and hope that a solution will come in the not-too-distant future. Meanwhile we must make the best of what assets we have. My proposal for constitutional reform tries to do just that. I suspect that most of my readers will feel that the gentlemen who met in Philadelphia so many years ago solved most of the problems here. I joined in the admiration for them but feel that now we know more and could do better.

Notes

1. Personally, I find keeping our troops in heavy clothing in that climate rather offensive. When the British occupied the area their troops wore shorts and short-sleeved shirts. I think ours should although they should carry with them protective clothing for the possible use of gas.
2. It is a history of various minor military actions undertaken by American

forces without a declaration of war. They have been widely forgotten in the United States but South Americans normally remember and resent those which took place in the western hemisphere.

3. The book has gone through a number of editions and publishers.
4. In England, the judge may rule 10 out of 12 adequate in some cases.
5. This chapter was written by me. Although the book is a joint product, parts of it were written by Buchanan or myself.
6. 'Hare system of proportional representation', *Encyclopedia Americana*, vol. 19, p. 210 (1969).

References

Ansolabehere, Stephen, John de Figueiredo and James M. Snyder, Jr. (2003), 'Why is there so little money in U.S. politics', *Journal of Economic Perspectives*, **17** (1), 105–30.

Arrow, Kenneth J. (1950), 'A difficulty in the concept of social welfare', *Journal of Political Economy*, **58** (4), 328–46.

Black, D. and R.A. Newing (1951), *Committee Decisions with Complementary Valuation*, London: William Hodge.

Boot, Max (2002), *The Savage Wars of Peace*, New York: Basic Books.

Buchanan, James and Gordon Tullock (1965), *The Calculus of Consent*, Ann Arbor: University of Michigan Press.

Coase, Ronald (1960), 'The problem of social cost', *Journal of Law and Economics*, **3**, October, pp. 1–44.

Dawkings, Richard (1989), *The Selfish Gene*, Oxford: Oxford University Press.

De Waal, Frans (1992), *Chimpanzee Politics*, Cambridge, MA: Harvard University Press.

De Waal, Frans (1989), *Peacemaking Among Primates*, Baltimore, MD: Johns Hopkins University Press.

DeJoinville, Jean and Geoffrey Devillehardouin (1963), *Chronicles of the Crusades*, Baltimore, MD: Malboro Books.

Demsetz, Harold (1967), 'Toward a theory of property rights', *American Economic Review*, **57** (2), 347–59.

Easterly, William (2002), *The Elusive Quest for Growth*, Cambridge, MA: MIT Press.

Fleming, Thomas (2003), *The Illusion of Victory*, New York: Basic Books.

Gibbon, Edward (1932), *The Decline and Fall of the Roman Empire*, New York: Modern Library.

Hume, David (1870), *Essays, Literary, Moral and Political*, London: Ward Lock.

Krueger, Anne (1974), 'The political economic of the rent seeking society', *American Economic Review*, **64** (3), 291–303.

Lane, Frederic C. (1973), *Venice, A Maritime Republic*, Baltimore, MD: Johns Hopkins University Press.

Lewis, Bernard (1987), *Assassins*, New York: Basic Books.

Liebergott, Stanley (1976), *American Economy: Income, Wealth and Want*, Princeton, NJ: Princeton University Press.

Namier, Lewis Bernstein (1957), *The Structure of British Politics at the Accession of George III*, London: Macmillan/ New York: St. Martin's Press.

Olson, Mancur (1965), *Logic of Collective Action*, Cambridge, MA: Harvard University Press.

Olson, Mancur (1982), *The Rise and Decline of Nations*, New Haven, CT: Yale University Press.

Pigou, A.C. (1929), *The Economics of Welfare*, London: Macmillan.

Rawls, John (2001), *Justice as Fairness*, Cambridge, MA: Harvard University Press.

Schumpeter, Joseph A. (1942), *Capitalism, Socialism and Democracy*, New York: Harper.

Schumpeter, Joseph A. (1954), *History of Economic Analysis*, New York: Oxford University Press.

Smith, Adam (1902), *The Wealth of Nations*, New York: Collier.

Tullock, Gordon (ed.) (1961), *A Practical Guide for Ambitious Politicians, or Walsingham's Manual*, Columbia: University of South Carolina Press.

Tullock, Gordon (1967), 'The welfare costs of monopolies, tariffs and theft', *Western Economic Journal,* **5**, 224–32.

Tullock, Gordon (1969), 'Problems of majority voting', *Journal of Political Economy*, **67**, December, pp. 1–19.

Tullock, Gordon (1971), 'Inheritance justified', *Journal of Law and Economics*, **14** (2), October, pp. 465–74.

Tullock, Gordon (1984), The economics of British politics', *Economic Affairs*, **4** (2), pp. 5–6.

Tullock, Gordon (1987), *Autocracy*, Dordrecht, the Netherlands: Martinus Nijhoff.

Tullock, Gordon (1997), *The Economics of Income Redistribution*, Boston, MA: Kluwer.

Tullock, Gordon (1998), *On Voting*, Cheltenham, UK and Lyme, USA: Edward Elgar.

Tullock, Gordon (2002), 'The evolution of self sacrificing behaviour', *International Journal of Bioeconomics*, **4** (2), pp. 99–107.

Wittfogel, Karl (1957), *Oriental Despotism*, New Haven, CT: Yale University Press.

Index